Praise for *Why Johnny Can't Think*

"Much of what we are told to believe these days is so obviously wrong and stupid that only very intelligent people could ever persuade themselves it is true. Robert Whitaker takes aim at the American professor-priesthood that spreads this foolishness, and by the time he is finished not one liberal myth is still standing."

Jared Taylor, Editor, *American Renaissance*

"Bob Whitaker has penned a devastating attack on the racket that American academia has become. Every prospective college student should read this book, also every parent of every prospective college student before spending the thousands and sometimes tens of thousands it takes to obtain a college or university degree these days."

Steven Yates, Ph.D., contributing writer for *LewRockwell.com* and author of *Civil Wrongs: What Went Wrong With Affirmative Action*

"Bob Whitaker has a quick and unerring eye for the fake and the foolish. Every one of his short shots at the false idols of the left (and, sometimes, the right) cuts off another leg. His book is a must for any reader interested in the realities beneath the surfaces of politics, education, and culture."

- **Samuel Francis**, Syndicated Columnist

Also By Robert W. Whitaker

A Plague on Both Your Houses. Washington, Robert
B. Luce, Inc., 1976

The New Right Papers. edited by Robert W. Whitaker.
New York, St Martin's Press, 1982

Why Johnny Can't Think

America's Professor-Priesthood

Robert W. Whitaker

Foreword by Joe Sobran

Kudzu Media

North Augusta, SC

Foreword copyright © 2004 by Joe Sobran

Printed in the United States of America
First printing, 2004

Cover art by Sandra Stewart

Library of Congress Cataloging-in-Publication Data

Whitaker, Robert W.
   Why Johnny Can't Think: America's Professor-
Priesthood
   / Robert W. Whitaker
   p.   cm.
   ISBN 0-9729292-0-7
   1. Conservatism – United States. 2. Education –
United States. 3. Higher Education – United States
4. Politics – United States

This book is dedicated to the readers of WhitakerOnline.ORG.

You are proof that strong minds can outgrow their youthful indoctrination.

Contents

Foreword by Joe Sobran   viii

Introduction: On Campus I Want
Less Marxists And More
Revolutionaries   3

1 Are Professors People?   5

There Can Be No Serious Political
     Right That Is Not Revolutionary   7
No Student Ever Seriously
     Questions His Professors' Motives   13
Follow The Money   17
For Our Inquisition, Heredity Is
     Heresy   21
The Dogs That Never Bark   27
Is There Any Way To Discredit
     Those Who Are Always Wrong?   33

2 Hitler's Priesthood   39

Doctor Joseph Goebbels,
     Constructive Social Critic?   41
Who Is The God Of America's
     Established Religion?   45
"The Bell Curve" Was Part Of
     An Intellectual Glacier   49
Arguing Nature Over Nurture
     Got People Killed!   55

The Time When Talking To Social
   Science "Experts" Seriously Was
   An Innocent Mistake Is Long Past   59
Academia Must Be Defrocked And
   Defunded   63
And When Do We Want It? NOW!   67
Is It Cruel And Unusual To Ask
   Professors To Think?   69
The Professors' Perfectly Tame
   "Young Revolutionaries"   73
Professor-Priests Are Also
   Professor-Prophets   75
Got Pet Commies? Then Get Pet
   Nazis   77
Thugs   79
Do Young People Have To Be
   Dumb?   83

3 Only An Intellectual Revolution
   Can Create A Real Social Science   85

This Is Not The First Time
   So-Called "Intellectuals" Have
   Gone Around The Bend   87
Things are not All That Bad   91
Semmelweis Solutions   97
Servetus Solutions   99
The Redneck Theory of Disease   105
Another Quick Review: If You See
   That The Emperor Has No
   Clothes, You Are "Simplistic"   111
If You See The Emperor Has No
   Clothes You Are
   Anti-Intellectual   115
East Really is East; West Really
   is West   119

Knowledge Versus Wisdom   123
Priests And Professors Through
    History   127

4 The Fake Opposition Must Go!   129

If You Want To Be A "Conservative
    Spokesman" You'd Better Not
    Bark, Either   131
Respectable Conservatives: The
    Kept "Opposition"   135
Respectable Conservatives
    Worship The "Neos"   139
Forget Subtlety. The Problem Is
    Gross Dumbness   143

5 The Politically Correct Hate List   147

Political Correctness Is Nothing
    New   149
And Now A News Bulletin About
    Mammoths   153
Political Correctness Is A Game
    Of Trumps   155
The Politically Correct Hate List   157
Make Up Your Mind, Do It Now
    And Do It Quick   159
All Inquisitions Are Like This   161
Political Correctness Is Not Like
    A State Religion, It IS Our State
    Religion   165
An Established Religion Always
    Destroys Precisely What It
    Claims To Champion   169
Nonviolent Thugs   171

What Would We Do If Any Other
  Religion Took Over Our Schools?   173

6 How Leftists Will Fight Academic
  Reform   177

Academia Is Ready To Fail Its
  Second Test   179
After Stonewalling, Social
  Scientists Will Fall Back On
  "Self-Regulation"   183
What Is This So-Called
  "Self-Regulation?"   187
The Left Needs Regulation Just
  Like The Right Does   191
If You Want To Take Money From
  Children You Call Yourself An
  "Artist"   193
The Media Says "We're Just Too
  Good To Be True"   197
Hardy's Law   203
Liberal Hicks   205
Laurel And Hardy, Professors
  And The Media   207
The Olympic Champions Of
  "Shrewd"   211
It Is Time For Laughter, It Is
  Time For Fury   215

Foreword

Why Johnny Can't Think is an odd book, if you can even call it a book. Its tone, thesis, and style are defiantly anti-academic. Many would call it anti-intellectual – and so it is, if the life of the mind is equated with the people we call intellectuals. It doesn't rely on charts and statistics; it appeals to common sense.

A former professor himself, Bob Whitaker believes that formal education has become dangerous, and often fatal, to common sense. This is nothing new, but Americans believe so deeply in formal education that they routinely sacrifice their children's youth to it, often paying staggering amounts of money to shield them from the real world.

Bob reminds us that in the Middle Ages, the advance of science was retarded not by the ignorant, but by the learned. All educated people "knew" that heavy bodies fell faster than light ones, and that men had more teeth than women. The great Aristotle had said so. And educated people preferred the authority of Aristotle to the simplest experiments and observations, which could have told them that the great Aristotle was just plain wrong.

Today the sciences are taught on a sounder basis. But, says Whitaker, the "social" sciences are another matter. These "social" sciences are often directly contradicted by the hard sciences. They are built on ideas and theories that are not only unproven, but demonstrably and obviously false. Yet they are aggressively promoted by the academy, followed by the media and the government, and anyone who openly denies them can forget about a career in these institutions. Even real scientists are forced to bow to the idols of "social" science.

This system of modern dogmas, of superstitions passing for scientific knowledge form what is now called "Political Correctness," closely linked to "Multiculturalism." It trains the young to accept and parrot the notion that all races, cultures, sexes, and sexual practices are equal, and that it is a grave thought-crime to deny this. Political Correctness, like Aristotle's physics in the Middle Ages, is what every educated person "knows." And a huge class of professional educators is richly rewarded for teaching it.

True science is based on demonstration, not authority. But it is only authority that sustains – and enforces – the doctrines of Political Correctness. And this authority is supported by enormous amounts of public money.

As Whitaker reminds us, formal education is far and away the biggest industry in the United States. Americans pay trillions of dollars, in both taxes and private tuition, to have their children indoctrinated in a false and destructive ideology, which serves as the basis for a series of disastrous public policies. In Whitaker's words, "Nothing liberals do ever WORKS."

That bluntness is typical. You may feel that Whitaker could use a little more qualification, subtlety, and even statistical evidence here and there. But British understatement isn't his style.

For Bob Whitaker, nuance is something they do in Europe. He isn't really trying to prove anything. He's trying to make you open your eyes. He dares you to tell him he's wrong, when reality is there, big as life, to back him up. He never tries to be clever; he likes to say what is startlingly obvious — but, thanks to the code of Political Correctness, taboo.

Whitaker is at his funniest and most scathing when he discusses the liberal's most valuable ally: the "respectable" conservative, whose role is to reinforce liberalism by treating it with respect. This respect is what makes him "respectable." That is, wel-

come in the media as liberalism's loyal opposition.
The conservative who gives liberalism the horselaugh
it deserves quickly forfeits any hope of being invited
back. Whitaker long ago ceased being invited back.

Liberal programs don't just fail; they backfire,
aggravating the problems they are meant to solve and
destroying the things they are supposed to improve.
But they are rarely repealed. They become en-
trenched, and the public, "educated" to accept the
authority of liberalism, forgets how much better many
things were before liberalism started improving them.

Unlike "respectable" conservatives, Whitaker re-
members. He sees. And he laughs.

Joseph Sobran

Introduction

On Campus I Want Less Marxists And More Revolutionaries

My immediate goal in writing this book is to see more students give their professors a hard time. When it comes to the social sciences, nobody on campus has to think. You get a degree by hopping through hoops and proving that you "fit in."

Today's campus has a group of perfectly tame students who call themselves "revolutionaries" because their hero Karl Marx was revolutionary. But that was in 1848. The novelty has worn off of Marx and of Marxism.

On the other side a few carefully chosen "conservatives" are allowed to speak on campus and in the media.

Our so-called National Dialogue is like an Oriental play where each actor has a mask on to tell you all about him: Sad Face, Happy Face, Angry Face. We have our Conservative, our Revolutionary Marxist, our Thoughtful Liberal, our Moderate, and so forth. Everybody above the age of fourteen already knows exactly what they are going to say.

Life is short and campuses are boring. This is because students quickly learn Rule One: if you want to fit in on campus, don't think.

Let's see if we can't shake that up a little.

Part One
Are Professors People?

There Can Be No Serious Political Right That Is Not Revolutionary

What we call "the political left" is nothing but a consistent drive to turn the world over to those who call themselves "intellectuals."

The much-touted leftist Love for the Working Class boils down to power for the "intellectuals." The "intellectual's" ideal philosopher, Karl Marx, said he did everything for the workers, but he never said the masses should rule. Marx wanted a "dictatorship of the proletariat."

And who would the "dictators of the proletariat" be?

Surprise, surprise, Karl Marx's "dictatorship of the proletariat" would not have a single working man in it! Marx's ideal was for "intellectuals" to rule over the workers.

Those who say they are professional intellectuals love Karl Marx.

Marx never did a day's work in his life. Lenin and Trotsky never did a day's work in their lives.

The first time I heard the Preamble to the Soviet Constitution was when a professor read it in class. I laughed out loud. Nobody else saw the joke.

That Preamble said that the Soviet Union would be "a nation of "workers, peasants, soldiers, AND INTELLECTUALS."

No ten-year-old would fall for that crap.

Let's say that several ten-year-olds were talking about setting up a country. One of the kids says, "OK, Tommy, You'll be the soldier. You'll do the fighting and get your leg blown off. Will, you'll be the peasant. You'll spend your whole day out in the mud and grow all our food. Frank, you'll be the worker. You'll spend all day in the factory."

Naturally, being intelligent ten-year-olds, Tom and Will and Frank will ask, "So what will you be doing?"

To which the guy setting things up will reply, "I'll be the intellectual. I'll sit around and tell you what to do."

No reasonably intelligent ten-year-old would be taken in by that line.

But leftist intellectuals never question that line. A room full of students in class with me saw nothing funny about it.

I laughed out loud.

I laughed out loud because I was more than ten years old and I had a mind to prove it.

It had never occurred to the rest of my class that there was anything funny about this crap.

It certainly never occurred to my professor that there was anything funny about this crap.

Liberals accept this pure unmitigated horseshit about rule by the intellectuals with a perfectly straight face.

If you list the villains of Political Correctness you will find that each and every one of them is a group that has money or power that the social science "intellectuals" want for themselves. Businessmen are evil, white people are evil, military men are evil, and so forth.

Leftism says that the money and power white people have needs to be taken in the name of White Guilt.

The government will take that White Guilt money. Then the only truly moral people in our society, the "intellectuals," will hand out that money.

Surely you didn't think minorities would decide how to hand out White Guilt money?

Businessmen also have money the "intellectuals" want to control.

Military men compete with professors for government money.

Anyone who is a villain of political correctness is in competition with those who call themselves "intellectuals." But no liberal ever notices this.

Leftists have a mental age of six.

My brother was literate when he was six, and it got him into trouble.

When my brother was six, my mother was pregnant with her fifth child, your obedient servant the author of this screed. During that fifth pregnancy my six-year-old brother read a fateful sentence in The Readers' Digest.

When you are six, no matter how smart you are, adults know everything and the printed word is sacred. And the printed words he read were:

"Every fifth child in the world is Chinese."

What the Reader's Digest meant was that one in five children on earth were Chinese.

But that is not what it SAID.

Sometimes my brother looked forward to the idea of a Chinese little brother. Sometimes it worried him. Soon he would be taking a little brother around who looked like absolutely nobody else he knew.

But the one thing he had no doubt about was that his little brother would have dark skin and epicanthic eye folds like any other little Chinese fifth child did.

The Reader's Digest had said so.

But no permanent harm was done because my brother grew up.

My brother was six years old, but he grew out of it.

A leftist is an adult who never grew out of it.

Leftists are six-year-olds mentally.

Meanwhile you can't be a "conservative spokesman" if you have a mental age above ten years.

All "conservative spokesmen" must have two things in common:

1) A "conservative spokesman" must be smart enough to hear the Preamble to the Soviet Constitution and smell a rat in there somewhere. In other words, they have to have the smarts of an average ten-year-old.

2) But you can't be a conservative spokesman if you are smarter than the average ten-year-old. A grownup that heard the Preamble to the Soviet Constitution would laugh out loud.

If you want to appear on talk shows as a Conservative Spokesman, you can't just laugh out loud at the Liberal Spokesmen on the other side.

You can't be a Conservative Spokesman if you see anything funny about Leftist Intellectuals who say professors should rule the world.

So today's adult world has no serious political right. Our National Dialogue consists of a left which says professors should rule the world and an opposition on the right which has to take them seriously.

Universities give leftism a solid base of power.

Since everyone who goes to college gets a thorough introduction to the idea that professors should rule the world, that idea exerts a lot of control. Our committed liberals include tens of millions of yuppies and pseudo-intellectuals who never outgrew their college education.

These millions of yuppies and pseudo-intellectuals who never outgrew their college education are referred to collectively as Fashionable Opinion.

Some open opposition to Fashionable Leftism is allowed. But it can only go so far.

How long would a talk show last if an adult got on it and laughed out loud at leftists?

So what we have is the left and a loose group of

libertarians, neoconservatives, Buckley theologues, and others who oppose leftism.

But every one of this hodge-podge of professional anti-leftists has to take leftism seriously. If you don't take leftism seriously, you don't get paid.

We cannot have a serious national dialogue until we stop this childishness.

No real right can exist unless it sweeps the silliness of the left away. No serious right can exist without starting by throwing every single Absolute, Required Truth that leftism preaches right out the window and starting fresh.

No adult right can take the left seriously. No political adulthood can exist unless its first demand is that we get rid of the unmitigated crap and start fresh.

No adult right can be respectable. It must be revolutionary.

No Student Ever Seriously Questions His Professors' Motives

I have spent many thousands of hours as a professor, as a student, and in public discussions. I have heard professors talk about how greedy businessmen are. I have heard professors talk about how power-hungry military men are.

But in all those hours I have never heard a word, and I mean not a WORD, about whether a professor might have professional biases of his own.

Military men have biases, even the best of them. A man can win a Medal of Honor risking his life to save others and be the most proven of patriots. But we have a healthy distrust of that same Medal of Honor winner if he is a professional soldier and is making policy recommendations.

If a man has spent his entire life in and near the oil industry, you have to assume he has some predictable biases you have to watch out for, even if he is the President of the United States.

The Bible of private enterprise is "The Wealth of Nations." It was written by Adam Smith in 1776. But even in that book Smith made it clear that the minute businessmen got together they began to conspire to fix prices.

In 1900, big businessmen were fixing prices nationwide. They had a label for anybody who denied their right to do this. In 1900, opponents of price fixing were called "socialists."

You cannot let businessmen do anything they want to in the name of Free Enterprise. If you do, you are courting disaster.

You cannot let military men do anything they want to in the name of Patriotism. If you do, you are courting disaster.

Today we are letting professors do anything they want to in the name of Academic Freedom. So they use the term "academic freedom" to suppress anything they don't like.

No student in any classroom ever even dreams of asking whether professors as a group have any greed or any biases or any hates. So professors are free to say that only white gentiles hate, that only businessmen are greedy, that only generals love war.

Only professors are without greed. Only professors are without biases. Only professors do not hate. Only professors want peace rather than war.

I cannot believe that a room full of literate people can take all this for granted. But they do. I have never seen a room full of literate people who did not take it for granted that professors are the perfectly objective, perfectly neutral observers of all other occupations.

The occupation of college professor is an occupation. The finest professor in the world has certain biases that come straight out of his profession.

Every human being has professional prejudices, no matter how idealistic he may be.

The most patriotic general in the world has dangerous professional biases simply because he is a professional soldier. A doctor who faces death regularly to deal with disease still has professional biases, no matter how brave and dedicated he is.

In fact, the more genuinely patriotic or dedicated a person is, the less likely he is to realize that he has professional prejudices. Every leftist professor thinks he is a pure intellectual. I never met a single leftist professor who even dreamed that his occupation could not be trusted to judge the rest of the world from a unique perch of pure wisdom.

If you trust businessmen with the economy you

will get stagnation by price-fixing. If you trust generals to make all foreign policy, you are playing with suicide.

Trusting people to be free of professional prejudice is not just a bad idea, it is suicidal.

This is because every occupation has its favorite ideology. This is because every occupation will go nuts if it is not regulated from the outside.

Does this include college professors?

What part of the word "every" are you having trouble with?

Follow The Money

Students hear their professors say, "Follow the money" when it comes to how greedy businessmen are. Students hear media commentators say "Follow the money" when it comes to how greedy oilmen or defense contractors are.

So why do professors ignore the fact that black Africans were as guilty of selling black slaves as white slave-traders were of buying them? Could it be that they are just following the money?

If you follow the money, it is obvious that white Americans have lots of money you can get out of them by making them feel guilty. Black Africans have none. If you follow the money, White Guilt is useful and black African guilt is not.

But every college graduate believes that only the right follows the money. The left itself is never accused of following the money.

A college graduate who never outgrew his diploma cannot imagine that professors might have a bias. He cannot imagine that professors follow the money. For example, professors follow the money when it comes to Guilt.

Hitler killed several million Jews. Stalin killed tens of millions of Russian peasants. Nobody mentions the peasants Stalin killed and every other motion picture is about the Jews Hitler killed.

There is money in dead Jews. There is not a dime in dead Russian peasants.

In 2003 Norman Finkelstein published a book called "The Holocaust Industry." The title alone speaks volumes. "The Holocaust Industry" goes into enormous detail about the pure money-and-power group that is STILL cashing in on Hitler.

Norman Finkelstein is not anti-Semitic. He is a Jew who is sick and tired of the exploitation of the Jewish dead. The loudest denunciations of "The Holocaust Industry" came from German leftists for whom Hitler is their bread and butter.

It just so happens that there is a vast stream of money in Hitler and not a dime in Stalin.

What we have here is people acting like people. Professors are an inbred self-selecting group of people with a professional bias. Due to their shouts of Academic Freedom there are no safeguards against the inbred fraternity of professors going ape.

So professors have gone ape.

This is not Evil Incarnate. This is as inevitable as gravity.

Stalin can kill all the Russian peasants he wants and no one cares, because no one gets paid for caring. Stalin committed leftist crimes, and neither academia nor Fashionable Opinion is interested in leftist crimes. Talking about leftist crime does not lead where Fashionable Opinion wants to go.

When white-ruled South Africa had apartheid, one of the country's big problems was keeping black immigrants OUT. If blacks in South Africa were poor by European standards they were rich by African standards. If they had few rights in South Africa they had NO rights in black-ruled countries.

So why was South Africa the only villain of Political Correctness in Africa?

If you say this was "leftist bias," you are only partly right. The reason South Africa was Evil Incarnate was because a lot of people made their livings off protesting about white South Africa. Nobody who gives out money gives a damn about one more starving black country ruled by one more black tyrant.

When you say "leftist bias" you are acting as if

leftism comes out of nowhere. Today's leftism is a result of professors and the people who never out-grew their college education acting predictably.

If you say "Professors are leftist," you've got it backwards. Leftism is the concept that "Professors should rule the world."

For Our Inquisition, Heredity Is Heresy

Social scientists are for nurture over nature. Social scientists want all social and economic problems to be entirely the result of a lack of the proper education, the proper sociology, the proper psychology, the proper history, the right philosophy. In other words, what we call "nurture" as opposed to "nature" happens to be exactly the same thing we call "social science!"

Given this fact it is not surprising that our totally inbred social sciences always come down on the side of nurture as opposed to nature. Your "college education" taught you that progressive thought is entirely on the side of environment over heredity.

Social scientists taught you that religiously.

I wonder why?

Well, DUHHH!

If you had had any serious education at all, a real education that taught you to think, that would have been obvious.

In the 1950s, when you said "the environment," you meant environment as opposed to heredity. You also meant the social scientist's stock in trade. A human being's abilities come from his heredity and his environment. Social scientists get any money and power they have entirely from the latter.

If everything were hereditary, social science would be totally impotent.

What we call "the environment" in this sense is all the things social scientists specialize in. A person is born with his genes. You only pay money to social scientists to get him educated, well fed, and raised according to all the latest ideas on parenting.

This meaning of "environment," as opposed to heredity, is what social science is all about. Everything that is not social science is a matter of genes or bodily chemistry. Genes and body chemistry are not what social scientists deal with.

On campus, social experts teach that genes are nothing and environment is everything.

In our day "the environment" means clean air, clean water, jungles – now called rain forests – and such like. On every campus, social science professors teach that evil businessmen and farmers and others are greedy and only social science professors are selfless and good. We need bureaucrats to run the economy according to plans laid down by social scientists if we are to save the world.

"Environment." Professors love that word.

There are two different meanings of the word "environment," but if an academic lynch mob is coming after you, you can just shout "Environment!" at them and save yourself some violence.

Academia believes what it wants to believe.

Those who never outgrow their college education believe what their professors want them to believe.

Everybody tends to believe what they want to believe. But in academia this tendency to state anything you want to believe as a fact goes unchecked. Like any other self-contained bureaucracy which is allowed to declare anything it wants to be a fact, academia has gone absolutely bonkers.

Here is how your professor was selected:

Many years ago, students who said what professors wanted to hear were selected to be professors. Professors decided who got their graduate degrees. Professors decided which of the younger professors got tenure.

These new professors in their turn selected professors in the next generation who believed even more firmly that professors who call themselves "intellectuals" should rule the world.

The result of this inbreeding is the totally intolerant leftist campus of today where nobody thinks he is intolerant at all.

To illustrate this, let us look at some of the truly insane "facts" that have been accepted by academics and then by the media.

No matter how ridiculous it is, an idea that sounds good to leftists will get repeated and go from academics to the media and be accepted as a "fact."

Everybody has forgotten one "fact" that the media pushed hard during the Carter Administration. Back then gays were trying to get gay families recognized as legitimate "families" by the Federal government.

Academics had to come up with a "fact" to back the gay position. To accomplish this they, like Sherlock Holmes, had "A Seven Percent Solution."

All the liberals said that only 7% of American families were "traditional families!"

Wow. That meant that homosexual couplings were just a part of the 93% of families that were not traditional. Everybody repeated that, on campus, in the news, in magazines.

I was working on Capitol Hill at the time, so I looked up this "93%" nonsense. The Labor Department in one study had said that what the average American thinks of as a traditional family is a married couple in which only the man works and they have one boy and one girl in a particular age group.

Only seven percent of American families have a working husband, a nonworking wife, and exactly one boy and exactly one girl in the right age group.

That is a little different from the implication that unwed mothers and homosexuals made up 93% of American families.

I wrote this into a speech my congressman gave and this "fact" not only disappeared, it has never been heard from since.

The "traditional family" seven percent solution was not a plot. It was simply the natural result of a hothouse environment. One person quoted the Labor Department's term "traditional family" and said it was seven percent. That part sounded good so all of academia took up the cry.

There was no one to correct them. Correcting the term when it got out of hand would be called anti-gay.

So the media repeated this line mindlessly.

I have been dealing with academic "facts" like the seven-percent traditional family bit for forty years. Anything that is too good for social science to pass up becomes a "fact." No one dares to challenge it because liberals will scream "Nazi!" or "gay-basher" or whatever. It becomes Fashionable Opinion and the media unquestioningly report it.

Respectable conservatives take this new "fact" seriously.

Here is another example of this kind of "fact:"

Leftism wants all guns in the hands of the state. Crime is to be taken care of by a Crime Policy formulated by criminologists. No citizen has a right to defend himself. That must be left to the Authorities. So when it comes to gun control some really crazy stuff passes for truth on campus and therefore in the media.

An example of this was the "43-1" myth. Professors taught, and the media repeated for years, that a person who tried to defend himself with his gun at home was FORTY-THREE TIMES as likely to have the intruder take that gun and kill him with it as he was to use it against the intruder.

You can't find anyone now who will admit they

ever said that, but it was an accepted "fact" for a long time.

Finally a few career cops started writing to newspapers about this 43-1 "fact." They said that they didn't know of a single instance where the brave burglar took the gun from a trembling householder and shot him with it. On the contrary, they knew lots of instances where burglars were shot or driven off by an armed citizen.

Actually, if you just think about it, this idea of the gun owner's being shot 43 times every time a burglar got shot is insane on its face. But it was reported and accepted as fact. Someone said it and it sounded good. Until those policemen stepped forward anybody who challenged this 43-1 nonsense was called a "gun nut."

The examples of such absurd academic "facts" are legion. My point is that if the political left wants frogs to have hooves, ten thousand professors will immediately sign a statement that frogs have hooves.

When I said that professors would declare that frogs have hooves if liberals want them to, I did overstate a bit, but even this is not that much of an overstatement. Read on and you will see what I mean in bloody and specific detail. If the left needs it, professors will testify to it.

But one thing at a time. To take our topics in order, it has taken this long just to introduce the reader to the novel idea that a professor might be a mere human being with professional biases. The idea that professors are just another occupational group is so radical it is hard to talk about.

I did not just say that every professor has a political view of his own. What nobody seems to realize is that professors, as an occupation, have general biases.

We all know about leftist bias on campus, but

we never ACT like we know about it. Every time another thousand professors come up with another declaration that something leftists want to believe is a "fact," everybody treats it as if it were an honest, impartial testimony that needs serious consideration. It is not.   Any statement by professors in support of the political left is as suspect as any statement by a professional military man on military expenditures.

It is time for us to stop being a bunch of political hayseeds and to start calling academia's predictable leftist declarations "Horseshit!" If you already know what someone is going to say, it's time to make them prove it, and not give them ANY benefit of the doubt.

The burden of proof is on academia because they have lied so freely for so long.

The Dogs That Never Bark

You won't see any scandals in the press about the power and money titans who rule the media.

If that simple sentence doesn't start the reader thinking, nothing can. A person who is not set to thinking by the simple mention of the lack of scandal in the media will never outgrow his college education.

There are plenty of reports of scams in military contracting. There are lots of rumors of oil companies doing wrong.

But when the money and power moves take place on the left, there is never the slightest hint of wrongdoing.

The hard left took over the Ford Foundation. Not a hint of anything wrong came from the media. The hard left took over other billion-dollar foundations. If the right took one major foundation over, everybody would know about it and there would be some discussion of possible problems. But there is never any mention of suspicion in the press when leftists take control of yet another gigantic private foundation.

If leftists are people, there must be just as much scandal with their money and power moves as there is in the money and power big business and military contractors have.

Are leftists people? If you have not outgrown your college education this question would never occur to you.

For the first time in history a national industrial takeover is occurring without a breath of scandal, without a hint of dishonesty.

There used to be hundreds of separately owned

local newspapers in America. These small businesses had a general bias to the political right. In every city these local newspapers are being taken over by national chains, all of which have a left bias.

If oil companies were taking over every local gas station, the media would watch them closely. In such a gigantic national takeover one might expect there to be some undue pressure, a little greed, maybe even a hint of outright viciousness somewhere in this coast-to-coast process.

In the national media takeover there has not been a hint of such problems. Conservative spokesmen are as desperate as liberal spokesmen to insist that every single big money man in the national media takeover is one hundred percent fair.

If the media are our watchdogs, why don't they ever bark at the left? Why do they agree that "intellectuals" have no biases, that there is never any dirt to be dug out when big money foundations are taken over by ideologues?

As Sherlock Holmes said, the important thing was that the dog didn't bark. Enormous power grabs constantly take place on the left, but there is never a hint of scandal about them in the media they control.

Not a HINT. Not a BREATH. Not a SUSPICION. Not a RUMOR. No barks, no whines. Hell, that dog never even wakes up.

If our media are watchdogs, why do they never bark at the biggest money and power industries in the world, education and the media itself?

And why doesn't anybody ever ask these questions?

"Saturday Night Live" is a favorite show of America's yuppies. Much of its humor is based on laughing at anyone who doesn't have Fashionable Opinions. But sometimes its humor really hits home.

On one show a college recruiter was holding a meeting of high school graduates who might go to his college. He closed the door and then made a proposition to the students. He said that if the kids would pay their tuition and fees, they could spend four years going anywhere they wanted to go and doing anything they wanted to do.

What made the skit funny was that it made sense. All you go to college for is a diploma. At the end of four years professors who are given the authority by government sign a diploma for you. There is no way to tell whether somebody actually went to college.

It doesn't matter if anybody went to college if they have the diploma. When you get right down to it, professors don't have to do anything but sign that piece of paper and please each other.

You talk about scandals. That is the elephant in America's living room.

If that skit had been presented to anything but a nation of college graduates, someone may have started thinking. Fortunately, when it comes to Young Upwardly Mobile Professional People, yuppies, there is no threat that they are going to start thinking.

A generation ago a lot of colleges admitted they were just diploma factories and abolished required courses altogether. You paid your money, jumped your hoops, and in four years you got your government-sanctioned piece of paper.

All those watchdogs of the press are out there looking for fixes that involve money. But if you are waiting for the watchdogs of Public Opinion to mention the biggest money fraud in the world today, diploma money, plan to wait until after you take that ice-skating trip in Hell.

For a person who was in academia in the 1960s, if he has a mind, the recent discovery of the genetic defects that cause depression is fascinating. In the

1960s the big debate was whether there was "a genetic component" to schizophrenia.

Anybody who said schizophrenia was inherited back then was called a Nazi.

If you had predicted in 1955 that we would not only find that the disease is genetic, but that we would find the actual genes involved, you would have been considered nuts.

In fact, in 1955, what we now call schizophrenia did not even go by that name. It was called "the schizophrenic response." The reason it was called "the schizophrenic response" was that all real scientists had to make it clear that this was a psychological response, not a physical matter.

In 1955 you could get the usual thousand professors to sign a document declaring that schizophrenia was proven to have nothing to do with genes. It was one of those academic "facts."

This absolute doctrine that schizophrenia and depression were "responses" had a hugely practical application. Depression and schizophrenia were the main subjects of the "science" of psychoanalysis. They were, in short, a billion-dollar industry.

The main indication that depression and schizophrenia were not just "responses" came from the fact that psychoanalysis didn't WORK. When the first tranquilizers came out, studies were done to see if tranquilizers were effective.

Unlike psychoanalysis or social sciences like psychology, if you sell a drug and it doesn't yield provable results, you can go to prison. So in the 1950s they did a comparison of treating patients with sugar pills, psychoanalysis, and tranquilizers.

People seek treatment only when their depression or other problem is acute. The result is that most people get better without any treatment at all. So two out of three patients got better with psychoanalysis and two out of three got better when they were given nothing but sugar pills (placebos). As required by law, a much higher percentage had permanent improvement when they were treated with the new tranquilizer drug, meprobomate.

If meprobomate had no more effect than psychiatry in treating mental illness, anybody selling it as a cure would have gone to prison.

Let me repeat that: If meprobomate had shown the same failure that psychoanalysis showed, anyone asking money for it would have gone to prison. But you could get the usual ten thousand professors to sign a paper saying psychiatry was wonderful.

News reports said the new tranquilizers had worked. News reports did not say that psychoanalysis was a total and costly failure when applied to depression and "the schizophrenic response." So billions of dollars continued to go into useless psychoanalysis, while barely one percent of our mental health money went into trying to find the real causes of these diseases.

No news media were going to report anything that indicated that the "schizophrenic response" was genetic.

When it comes to genetics, professors and media always use the Hitler Dodge. A theory called parallel development in anthropology threatens the academic orthodoxy on race questions. The leading proponent of parallel development in today's anthropology stated flatly that he would never contradict racial orthodoxy because HITLER was a racist.

That falls a little short of a real scientific approach, but nobody is going to mention that.

If a scientist were to say that income redistribution and poverty had no effect on human progress because Stalin said it did, he would be discredited instantly. But it has been taken for granted that hu-

man genetics means Hitler, so there can be no serious human genetics. Now that we are finding the
actual specific genes that influence human behavior, that mythology is impossible to maintain.

So everybody has just conveniently forgotten the
anti-genetics mythology that a professor could be fired
for denying a few decades ago.

The story here is not in what is said, but in the
silence. The anthropologist cited above simply states
what he takes for granted. Nobody considered it the
slightest bit unusual that a scientist would declare
that his science is a product of his political orthodoxy.

The story of "the schizophrenic response" is in
the total silence about it. Once again the truth is
where Sherlock Holmes said to look for it, The Silence of the Dogs.

The most important message of our age is to be
found in the stories that are not told. It is time we
stopped being fashionable and started looking at the
story that the dogs that do not bark are telling us.

Is There Any Way To Discredit Those Who Are Always Wrong?

Those of us whose brains did not die in college are actually stunned by just how stupid academic ideas are.

All progress is based on experimentation. The left says they believe in "social experiments."

But nothing is an experiment if you refuse to accept the results.

Prohibition was a social experiment. Prohibition was called a social experiment when it was adopted.

Prohibition was a disaster. So we got rid of it. That is a true experiment.

Leftism has a string of disasters worse than Prohibition in every field of social endeavor. In the 1950s those who said they were "intellectuals" were almost universally agreed that socialism was "the wave of the future." On campus it was almost universally required doctrine that if the government owned and ran all industry, the result would be not only efficient but fair.

Government ownership of the means of production and distribution was not only efficient. It was also inevitable.

What this meant was that the "intellectual" would take over the economy.

The result was that the third world was ruled by "intellectual socialists" and two generations of people lived in stagnant poverty while one Five Year Plan after another failed. The human cost of that failure was staggering.

This was a hideous catastrophe, one of the greatest human catastrophes in history. No student hears about it in class. No one in the media discusses it.

Billions of people lived in misery and poverty in
the third world while economists trained at Harvard
and the London School of Economics tried socialism
decade after decade. Whole generations wasted their
lives under Communism, but even more people
wasted their lives while economists simply refused to
admit that the nonsense of third-world "democratic
socialism" did not work.

With the collapse of the Soviet Union most of the
third world began to adopt the market system. They
have made more progress in a few years than every
socialist economy on earth had made in the generations before.

The human cost of rule by the "intellectuals" was
incalculable. It was one of the greatest human trag-
edies in history.   But you will never hear about it in
the universities.

The destructive socialist absurdity that was de
rigueur on university campuses in the 1950s was a
direct result of professors claiming that they were
intellectuals and that they, the intellectuals, should
rule the world.

In the 1960s it was generally agreed among "intellectuals" that "so-called criminals" were actually
victims of society. All one needed to end crime was to
dump money into psychological programs, sociologi-
cal programs and education and the crime problem
would disappear.

In other words, the "intellectuals" should take
over the legal system.

The result of that policy was that felons were re-
peatedly let back out on the streets. The human cost
of this policy was staggering.

In the 1970s you were shunned on campus if
you believed that there were any genetic differences
in the behavior of men and women. If you took away
girls' dolls and boys' guns, the whole oppression of

females would end.

Yes, Virginia, they were serious. They were deadly serious. Any disagreement was chauvinism and Hitlerism. You paid dearly for it.

All that was needed was a huge infusion of money into sociology, psychology and education and women could go on to what John Galbraith called "the higher economic role of women."

Professors insisted that "It is as important for a woman to paint a picture as to have a baby." Many, many women followed that advice and lived to regret it bitterly.

Militant feminists do not like being reminded of their 1970s absurdities, so no respectable conservative ever mentions them.

I remember when every responsible voice in the media and on campus talked about "getting to the root causes of crime."

There was no such thing as a criminal. Criminals were victims. Society was to blame. All the hippies insisted that we just needed to spend many billions hiring social scientists to reform the System and there would be no crime.

These were the Young Revolutionaries. Their "Revolution" consisted of demanding that the world be handed over to their professors.

We tried turning crime over to liberal programs and the crime rate skyrocketed. We turned education over to the education professors and literacy collapsed.

Every time we adopt yet another fashionable social science idea it is a disaster. But the college graduates simply will not grow up and see this.

The result has been the imposition of one policy after another that has been a total failure. Modern educational theories that got rid of phonics are just a few of many more examples.

Social science professors love to say they are the only True Voice of Humanity. But in the world I live in most of the real catastrophes were the direct result of fashionable opinion that came straight out of the universities.

But no matter how often they fail, liberal professors remain convinced they are the embodiment of true wisdom and true compassion. Their students are taught this, and many never grow out of it.

The problem is that our social experts, our social science professors, are always wrong. But their mistakes are not the kind a person can respect, the way a respectable conservative has to respect social science professors in order to be labeled respectable in liberal eyes.

The time is long past when social science professors were making reasonable errors. They are now ridiculous and the only real opposition would be one that laughed outright at their absurdities.

We keep paying social scientists. The liberal media and respectable conservatives all take it for granted that we should always pay them and turn our children over to them to be "educated."

Until we learn to stop going to people who are always wrong because they have a degree conferred on them by their equally silly colleagues, we will continue to let them destroy us.

But is there any way, any way on earth, for Americans to understand that the fact that a group of people is always destructive is a reason that we should stop listening to them, paying them, trusting them, groveling before them, giving our children to them?

"But," the respectable conservatives say, "We have to respect social scientists' opinions because they have Ph.D.s."

There is not the slightest relationship between a Ph.D. in physics and a Ph.D. in sociology. If one single chemistry professor ever produced a theory that was just plain silly, he would not be long in his profession. If one single physicist ever produced a single theory that caused an atomic bomb to go off at the wrong moment and kill a dozen people at a test site, he would never hear the end of it.

But a few dozen people killed is chicken feed compared to the routine cost of yet another social science disaster.

And another and another and another.... ad infinitim?

Part Two
Hitler's Priesthood

Doctor Joseph Goebbels, Constructive Social Critic?

Dr. Joseph Goebbels was the head of Adolf Hitler's Ministry of Propaganda

Though he did not openly advocate genocide, Dr. Goebbels said Germany should somehow get rid of Jews and other minority groups. Before World War II, the Nazis discussed many ways of dealing with "the Jewish race."

Dr. Goebbels' goal was that of abolishing the Jewish race's presence in all the countries he saw as "Aryan" countries. One way to do this was to send the Jews to Africa or Asia and mix them in with the populations there.

Genocide or not, I think we all recognize that what Dr. Goebbels was pushing was Hate.

If you want to rid the world of minorities, you are a Hater.

If you want to rid the world of white gentiles, you are a Constructive Social Critic.

If you want to rid the world of minorities the way Dr. Goebbels did, you get executed as a Hater. If you want to rid the world of white gentiles, you are paid well as a Constructive Social Critic.

Dr. Noel Ignatiev is a paid Constructive Social Critic. Dr. Ignatiev is a professor at Harvard University in a chair fully financed by big business money. This Constructive Social Critic says:

"The goal of abolishing the white race is on its face so desirable that some may find it hard to believe that it could incur any opposition other than from committed white supremacists."

So Professor Ignatiev is a Constructive Social Critic and I am now under suspicion of being a racist. If you want to prove this to yourself, ask yourself a quick question. Is anybody going to get mad at Ignatiev for getting paid to push the abolition of the white race, or are conservatives who read this going to suspect that I am "a committed white racist?"

All respectable conservatives have to agree to abolishing the white race. They don't say it the way Ignatiev does, but every conservative and every liberal agrees 1) that the Third World must be encouraged to immigrate and integrate into EVERY white majority country; and

2) The Third World must be encouraged to immigrate and integrate ONLY into white majority countries. No one brings up Third World immigration into Japan (which is less crowded than the Netherlands), or into Taiwan or into the huge undeveloped regions of Africa.

Africa for the Africans, Asia for the Asians.

When liberals and professional conservatives get relaxed, they agree that intermarriage is the "solution to the RACE problem." But nobody talks about a "solution to the race problem" in Asia or Africa. The "solution to the race problem" means "the solution to the white problem," and we all know it.

So when Goebbels advocated the "solution to the Jewish problem" he was engaging in Hate. To prove you have no hate in you, you have to favor the "solution to the RACE problem."

This is too subtle for the average college graduate, but it's pretty easy to see through if you have normal intelligence. And once again, the only person who will be accused of Hate for mentioning this will be me.

Today, Constructive Criticism says that anyone in Europe who says that the white race deserves credit for anything, from wiping out smallpox to going to the Moon, is a racist.

Anything good is done by the Progress of Humanity. Good things are done by All Humanity, not by whites.

To quote directly from the script, "This is a small step for Man and a Giant Leap for Mankind."

But you are required to say that whites did everything evil, from the death of American Indians to African slavery to capitalist greed and beyond.

Dr. Goebbels admitted that Jews were shrewd, but he said all the advances Jews were credited with were stolen from others. Dr. Goebbels said the Jews were responsible for every evil thing that was done.

Every student is taught that whites do the world's evil and Mankind does all the good.

Dr. Ignatiev points out that this leads straight to the Final Solution to the White problem. To be a conservative spokesman, you have to agree with this, though they seldom come right out and say it the way Ignatiev does.

They use terms like "a multiracial Europe" or "a melting pot America." But the bottom line is that whites have to go.

Dr. Goebbels said that the bottom line was that the Jews had to go.

The Final Solution has not changed. The only question is which people you want the solution applied to.

Who Is The God Of America's Established Religion?

We who are part of the Christian, Moslem or Jewish tradition think of God as being good. But gods are not good in all religions.

The gods of ancient Greece were morally neutral. In the ancient Persian religion, Ahriman the god of evil was more or less equal to Mazda, the god of goodness.

Easter Island had family idols they called their aku-aku. The aku-aku had to be kept secret, but they were evil, and the islanders wanted to be rid of them.

Carthaginians burned children alive for the god Moloch. Not all gods have been good.

The god of Political Correctness is altogether evil.

The name of the god of Political Correctness is Adolf Hitler.

In a Christian or Moslem society God is the one on whom all truth depends. To discover what is true, we go to the utterances of our particular god. Anything which is of him is good, everything that is not of him is evil.

Our modern religion is Political Correctness. Political Correctness denounces all heresy in the name of Hitler. The only difference between Hitler's place in our modern established religion and Jesus in the Christian faith is that whatever Jesus was for is holy to Christians while everything Hitler said is unholy at our liberal seminaries, which we call universities.

Every evil is denounced at our liberal seminaries in the name of Hitler in exactly the same way that goodness is pronounced by Christians in the name of Jesus.

And as one liberal policy after another fails, liberals come more and more to rely on the name of Hitler to justify them.

For every person killed by Hitler in this century, twenty have been killed by Communists. But no one mentions the Communists except as an afterthought.

This is because the evil done by Communists is of no use to Fashionable Opinion. There are tens of billions of dollars in dead Jews. There is not a penny in dead Russians or Chinese or in dead Cambodian peasants.

If you follow the money, it leads you straight to Hitler.

The Americans who fought Hitler in World War II thought they were fighting against tyranny and mass murder. Our ally, Joseph Stalin, was even more a tyrant and mass murderer than Hitler was, so they didn't like to think about that.

Both Hitler and Stalin used tyranny and mass murder as the means to an end.

For the priests of today's established religion in America, it is not Hitler's dictatorial means and mass murder that made him the Evil One. It was Hitler's ENDS that made him the Satan of Political Correctness.

In the 1960s liberals openly admired Communist dictator Ho Chi Min just as they admire Fidel Castro today. They say that these men may have been tyrants and killers, but they did it all for idealistic ENDS.

Today every liberal says that Hitler was evil because he was a racist, not because he was a tyrant. Every respectable conservative has to agree.

In the eyes of our established religion True Evil in is not a matter of means like dictatorship and mass slaughter. For Political Correctness, evil is being for racism and against Social Progress. If you use dictatorship and mass slaughter to pursue Social Progress,

Political Correctness says you are just being too idealistic.

It is genetics in general and race in particular that are, to our ruling religion, the ultimate heresy.

This is because if genetics is important, social science professors can never rule the world.

"The Bell Curve" Was Part Of An Intellectual Glacier

Franz Boas died in 1944. Boas was a Columbia University professor who dedicated his entire life to the idea that all races are innately the same. For decades he argued that the only reason black IQ's were lower than white IQ's was because their environment was different. Oriental IQs in America were higher than whites and Orientals were definitely discriminated against, but Boas ignored that.

As a good leftist "intellectual," Boas ignored anything that didn't support his argument.

Boas was an immigrant from Prussia who had faced oppression in his homeland because he was a Jew. His fight for black equality was based on the concept that Jews were an oppressed minority. He wanted Jews to be the leaders in a coalition of oppressed minorities against white gentiles.

This is not a radical statement. In its discussion of Boas, Public Television pointed out that he was the leader in forming an alliance between Jews and blacks.

College anthropology texts in 1940 described Boas as something of a joke. Some agreed Boas had a point, but they argued that you could not take seriously the idea that the average inborn black IQ was equal to the white IQ.

Suddenly, in 1945, the Boas doctrine became Gospel, the Only True Faith, what we now call Political Correctness. Hitler had believed in racial inequality, so all those who opposed Hitler had to believe in Boas.

A paragraph began to appear in absolutely every kind of publication after 1945.

That paragraph read:

"Modern anthropologists (meaning Boas' group) have proven that all races are equal in innate abilities." It was in the Reader's Digest World Almanac. It was in social science texts. It was everywhere.

I particularly remember that paragraph when I saw it in a COMIC BOOK! It showed three runners, one black, one white and one Oriental, all hitting the finishing tape in a FOOT RACE at the same time. Underneath was the lesson:

"Modern anthropologists have proven that all races are equal in innate abilities."

Nowadays, if there is one thing we know about race, it is that West Africans and Bostonians are not equals in the Marathon.

But that sentence was everywhere, so we assumed it was correct. Just as today everyone has to agree that race does not exist, back then everybody had to agree that all races' innate abilities were equal.

In the 1950s, Nathaniel Weyl was writing a book called "The Negro in American Civilization." He wanted to affirm what everybody knew — that all races were equal in innate ability — for a quick quote in his book. So he looked for that proof that "modern anthropologists have proven that all races are equal in innate abilities." Weyl was astonished to discover that all the real evidence was the other way, so he made it a major point of his book.

Weyl thought he had discovered something startling that people would want to hear about!

In the real world, there never was the slightest hint of any evidence of any kind for Boas' theory. It simply had to be true because that was the way things had to be after World War II:

Hitler was a racist, so race couldn't matter.

So when Weyl wrote about his discovery that Boas had no case, he ran into a thunderstorm of attacks.

Weyl found out that Political Correctness is a religion that punishes anyone who doubts it. The only proof Political Correctness needs is the smell of burning heretics.

In the 1960s, Harvard Psychology Professor Arthur Jensen was asked to do an article for the "Harvard Educational Review." As a part of that article, he decided to dip into the proof that races were innately equal, which he knew, as everybody else did, was overwhelming. He found it wasn't there, and he considered this front-page news.

Jensen wrote a long article announcing this discovery. His article took up that whole issue of The Harvard Educational Review. He didn't realize it was verboten.

As you can imagine, the result was a loud and reverberating explosion from the entire academic community. As always, thousands of professors lined up to sign statements that this heresy was wrong.

What followed came straight out of the Inquisition. The Harvard Educational Review tried to get back all the issues it had printed with this heresy AND BURN THEM!

Sound familiar?

The editor of the Harvard Educational review begged forgiveness. Jensen kept arguing that what he said was just the truth. But the truth is no excuse for heresy.

Some years after Jensen, Nobel Prize winner William Shockley was looking for proof that the races were equal. Guess what HE came across and made into a sensation? Nobel Prize winner Crick did the same thing. They both got wildly denounced.

So when a book called "The Bell Curve" came out in the 1990s, co-authored by yet another psychology professor (Richard Herrnstein), which showed once again that whites and blacks are not, on the average, innately equal in IQ, the usual shriek of "heresy" came out again. Once again thousands of professors lined up to sign statements that it wasn't true.

When "The Bell Curve" came out, the reaction from the priests of Political Correctness was, as always, to burn the book and punish the offenders. My editor has a perfect illustration from his own personal experience. He wrote me:

"Bob,

"The year The Bell Curve came out I was a grad student in anthropology. I was in Atlanta at the American Anthropology Association annual meeting. I had not seen the book yet, but the anthropology world was abuzz with how horrible it was.

"Anyway, I was running the Harvard Press booth at the convention that year. Early on (this was a three or four day convention), a group of people led by this very tall and unattractive white feminist professor type spokesperson came over to the booth, surrounded it and started waving signs and shouting at everyone who passed to boycott my booth and denouncing The Bell Curve.

"I asked her what they were doing. She said that they were protesting The Bell Curve. I asked her if she had read it. She said no, with no trace of embarrassment in protesting a book she hadn't read. I then told her that Harvard Press was not the publisher. I explained to her that one author was a professor at Harvard. When they heard this, they moved to the booth where the actual publisher was located.

"Every time I walked by that booth, that group was there protesting. Very few if any of the protestors had even read the book, which turned out to be pretty tame and common sense, I thought, when I finally read it."

One leading anthropologist pointed out recently that HITLER said that there was a connection be-

tween genetics and a society's advancement, so any-
one who mentions this is someone who loves Nazi
Death Camps. He actually intended this as a SCIEN-
TIFIC reason to brush race aside.

By the way, it is interesting that my editor was
reporting from the convention of the American Anthropological Association. That group has a long history of censorship on racial issues.

The president of the American Anthropological
Association in 1962 was the world's leading physical
anthropologist, Dr. Carleton Coon. In that year they
voted to condemn his new book, "The Origin of Races,"
for racial heresy. Not surprisingly, he resigned his
chairmanship.

The fact that there is no evidence whatsoever in
favor of innate racial equality is a lot like a glacier. It
keeps coming to the surface. Everybody assumes that
since you are required to believe in innate racial equality there must be solid support for it. Whenever anyone happens to check it out, they think they have
discovered something new.

The fact that racial equality has no scientific basis whatsoever keeps coming to the top on a regular
basis, and those people who are paid to denounce
heresy against Political Correctness raise the same
shriek every time.

And, as always when Political Correctness needs
a thousand professors to denounce a heresy, they
are right there with bells on.

Arguing Nature Over Nurture Got People Killed!

What we call nurture, as opposed to nature, environment as opposed to heredity, is what the social sciences are all about. If you list the different parts of nurture: education, psychology, sociology, ideology and so forth, you are listing the social sciences.

The whole political left is dedicated to environment over heredity. Communism says that man will be completely transformed if the world adopts the Communist ideology. The biggest problem Communist theory runs into is that human nature is largely a result of heredity, something that ideology cannot touch any more than the social sciences can.

Until the 1930s Russian geneticists were organized in the Medicogenetical Institute of Moscow. The last act that Institute ever performed was to actually test nurture versus nature. They took A THOUSAND SETS of identical twins and separated them at birth into very widely differing environments. Since identical twins have exactly the same genes, all the differences between them would result from nurture, but all their similarities would be a result of their common nature.

Some identical twins were put in a low IQ environment while others were put into a high IQ environment. But when the Medicogenetical Institute tested the results, the identical twins had almost identical IQs!

As always, the tests showed that the identical twins were astonishingly similar. The reason poor parents have low IQ children is mostly because poor parents with low IQ's tend to have children with low IQs. The similarities between identical twins — including those separated at birth — in everything from their IQs and their talents to their choice of toothpaste is common knowledge now.

Proving that humans are the result of nature rather than nurture can get you fired on an American campus. But it can get you KILLED in a Communist country. So guess what happened to the Medicogenetical Institute?

An Oxford professor friend of mine was a geneticist of such note that he was a Fellow of the Royal Society. Not the Royal Society OF something. I mean THE Royal Society. He was a professor at Oxford University during the 1930s and he was a regular correspondent with a lot of the members of the Medicogenetical Institute of Moscow.

After the Medicogentical Institute came out with that study favoring nature over nurture, said my friend, they began to disappear without trace. One by one, he began to hear nothing from them and nothing about them.

Finally the president of the Medicogenetical Institute of Moscow publicly "confessed his ideological error and was shot."

After wiping out the Medicogenetical Institute, Stalin turned Soviet genetics over to a good Communist ideologue named Lysenko. Lysenko made nurture absolute over nature, he declared environment supreme over heredity. Lysenko, as Stalin's chief geneticist, declared that you could change summer wheat to winter wheat BY FREEZING IT! Wheat growing, said Lysenko, was nurture, not nature.

You can imagine what effect that thinking had on Soviet agriculture. Communism's New Genetics caused the same catastrophes American social science does, and for exactly the same reason.

Actually, all this makes you wonder just what the IQ of the average member of the Medicogenetical

Institute was. To come down on the side of heredity versus environment under Stalin, you had to be especially immune to reality!

Americans are nowhere near that naïve. Every student knows that you can fail a course if you come down too often on the side of heredity versus environment. Every professor knows you can ruin your career that way.

Every genetics professor knows you lose your job for coming out on the wrong side of the race issue. The social science faculty is huge and powerful. Anyone who will not toe the line on this issue will not get a job at any leading university, if he gets any job at all, whether he teaches genetics or engineering or political science.

Everybody who has made it through graduate school and the years on the faculty needed to get tenure has passed this test. So it is always a shock when yet another professors looks up what he assumed to be proven fact and finds the emperor is as naked as a jaybird and backed only by academic thuggery.

Yes, Virginia, I said academia is now a bunch of thugs. Those screaming lynch mobs on campus who threaten anyone who is not Politically Correct are only different from the lynch mobs of old Mississippi because our modern communications make it impossible to actually lynch somebody and get away with it.

The other difference is that we did not pay for the old Mississippi lynch mobs with our tax dollars. You were not part of the old lynch mobs, but every American pays for the new ones.

There is nothing harmless about what our Politically Correct priesthood calls "idealism." Far, far more people have died in the name of environmentalism than Hitler killed in the name of racism.

The Time When Talking To Social Science "Experts" Seriously Was An Innocent Mistake Is Long Past

If you ask an education professor whether IQ's differ because of education or because of genes, he will tell you to give him enough money and power and he will cure most IQ differences through education.

Not long ago if you asked a psychologist whether any mental illness is the result of brain chemistry or a purely psychological problem, he would tell you he only needs you to give him money and power over the patient to cure that mental illness.

But today, even a genetics professor can't save a psychology professor from looking ridiculous if the psychologist says what he really wants to say about heredity or the chemistry of the brain. Today, even university psychologists have to give SOME credence to heredity and brain chemistry. Naturally everybody has agreed to forget the insane position all social scientists took on these issues just a few years ago.

Especially the media.

If you ask a criminologist whether crime is a matter of nurture or nature, he will still tell you, as much as possible, that the whole answer is nurture, i.e., criminology. Twenty years ago he still claimed that criminality was ENTIRELY a matter of nurture, something for social scientists to deal with.

Since then we have not only found many genetic patterns, we have found the very genes they can be traced to. Even college students are not dumb enough to swallow the old 99% nurture line today.

But still, if you ask the criminologist, he will demand that almost all the money used to end crime be spent on his "rehabilitation" programs.

By a strange coincidence, "rehabilitation" is the one field that still belongs entirely to the criminologist. He will say a few words about genetics and the chemistry of the brain, but as few as he can get away with.

Every long discussion of social policy concludes with some quick words to the effect that, "Genes matter, too," but no student in America can tell you any discussion he ever heard in any class that ever went any further than that on the subject of heredity.

In fact, the only other thing you will hear about heredity in any college classroom will be propaganda to discredit it and call ideas of heredity Hitlerite.

On the modern American campus there is a lot of prattle about questioning one's professors, but there is no serious questioning of professors where it counts.

The last thing you will ever hear in any classroom is any student asking about heredity.

And believe me, their new bows in the direction of brain chemistry and heredity do not make the recommendations of social scientists and criminologists the least bit less disastrous. Liberal recommendations forced courts to keep the mentally ill who are homeless on the streets. Social scientists' policies also keep as many criminals as possible on the streets, too.

Catholic Church authorities have been whining that they are innocent of all those rapes of little boys that priests committed. Their excuse is that back when most of that happened they were just following orders.

The Catholic authorities openly insist that, back when they ignored child molesters, every single social expert from the universities told them that these people should be "rehabilitated." But every other recommendation of those social science "experts" had already been a catastrophe and the Catholic Church listened to them anyway. That is inexcusable.

The Church is right about one thing: that rehabilitation line is what every trendy university professor recommended. But then, as now, nothing they say ever WORKS.

Tomorrow's crimes will be committed because we listened to those social "experts" AGAIN.

No respectable conservative ever points out that the social "experts" are always wrong. I understand why this is true. I understand how desperately conservatives want that "respectable" label. But if they continue to treat "professors should rule the world" as a viewpoint worthy of respect they are as guilty of the results as Catholic bishops were in the cases of child molestation by priests.

If you listen to leftist professors, you will become a criminal, too. The time when listening to social "experts" was an honest mistake is long, long past.

Academia Must Be Defrocked And Defunded

Social science professors hold the same positions in our established religion of Political Correctness that priests held in the Medieval Church. For anything from a civil service job to an army commission and beyond the government requires that a person be approved by professors and granted a degree.

Private businesses now enforce that same professorial monopoly by requiring college degrees. Those degrees are a monopoly of the professors.

No professor has to produce anything. He just has to sign a degree to make his living.

No professor has to please anybody but other professors. In academia, it is "publish or perish." But who decides who gets published? The professors who run the journals decide. Who decides which person gets a doctor's degree so he can become a professor? Other professors, of course. Who decides which professors get tenure? Other professors, of course.

The only thing professors have to do for the public is sign the degree you must have for professional survival.

Like Medieval priests, social scientists are selected entirely by other professors and then given lifetime tenure. Government money is used to hire them as our Official Experts.

Like Medieval priests, social science professors are given access to our children and are made our national judges. Like Medieval priests, they are paid to tell us how guilty we are and to tell us what programs we must pay for and what groveling we have to do to expiate our sins as white people and Americans.

And a social scientist is no more expected to produce observable results than was a medieval priest. They need give no evidence for their faith.

The only answer to this incredible and inexcusable state of affairs is for us to take away every vestige of priesthood social science professors have been given.

When colleges abolished required courses, we continued to require their degrees for young people to advance. The courses didn't matter, all that was needed was for professors to sign the degree. For degree signing, once again, only inbred academia has authority. Accreditation is given by one group of academic priests to another group.

Accreditation must be abolished and replaced by some method that holds professors responsible.

In other words, our priesthood must be defrocked.

Again, our Politically Correct priesthood is funded by public money. Again, only professors determine who will be admitted to that priesthood.

Nor is this payment entirely in the form of money. Even television stations are required to devote valuable time to Politically Correct theology in the form of Public Service Messages. Almost every charity has to give at least a part of its money to groups sponsoring leftist propaganda.

When the United Way raised money specifically for September 11 victims and immediately gave part of it to an "anti-Hate Project," Bill O'Reilly protested. But the fact is that every charity, if it wants to keep its tax-deductible status, is well advised to give money first to some kind of Politically Correct propaganda program.

This is outrageous, but these hundreds of millions of dollars of charitable tithes required for our established religion are comparatively minor compared to the rest of the PC scam.

So let's keep our eye on the prize. We spend hundreds of billions in government money on programs in the fields ruled by the priesthood of social science. This self-selected priesthood gets its share of every dollar and every bit of power those programs produce.

Unlike real scientists, social scientists need produce no results at all. Nothing they recommend works. So they just demand more. Like any other established priesthood all they offer us is a faith that punishes all disagreement.

This priesthood is all right for Europeans. Europeans have always been ruled by some kind of priesthood and they expect it. But, for America, this established religion and its priesthood is both humiliating and inexcusable.

It is time for America's Politically Correct priesthood to be defrocked and defunded.

And When Do We Want It? NOW!

When I listen to a social science professor drone his orthodoxy, I do not think about how I am offended by his opinions. I have spent a lifetime in politics. Listening to sillyass drivel doesn't bother me.

What I resent is not the professor's opinions.

I resent his lunch.

I paid for it.

I resent his suit.

I paid for it.

I resent his shoes.

I paid for them.

I resent PAYING for his drivel.

P.G. Wodehouse wrote hilarious books about Bertie Wooster and his butler, Jeeves. In one book Bertie Wooster has had to hire another butler for a while. The butler is a drunk and Bertie is hiding from him in the bushes while the butler runs around the house yelling with a butcher knife in his hand.

While he is watching this from the bushes, Bertie says, "You know, I haven't had a chance to fire him."

"So what?" says a guy hiding in the bushes with Bertie.

"Well," says Bertie, "I have to give him two week's notice from the time I fire him. So if you think about it, I am actually paying him right now to run around after me with a butcher knife."

I may find the political opinions of a congressman despicable, but he got elected to have them. I don't like opposition political ads, but if they collect the money to run them, I will fight for their right to do so.

When the government forces me to pay money

for someone to push his own political agenda, I will fight just as hard to STOP him from doing it.

I am a white gentile, and I am sick and tired of paying professors to run around trying to get rid of us. I am sick and tired of paying for leftist seminaries that call themselves Universities. I am sick and tired of paying for a monopoly in which professors take my money for a game they are playing with themselves.

I demand that this costly destructive tyranny end. I want a real revolution, a revolution against this insanity. And I want it now.

Is It Cruel And Unusual To Ask Professors To Think?

I don't resent the social scientists' ideas. I do resent their lunch, which I pay for, I resent their clothes, which I pay for. Professors sit in the clothes I paid for digesting the lunch I paid for and they say I am trying to crush their academic freedom.

When I represented the taxpayers as a member of the senior staff of the ~~~~House~~~~~~~~~~~~~~~~ ~~~~Education and Labor Committee – Damn, that sounds impressive! – I found that college graduates take it for granted that taxpayers should be forced to pay for the professor's lunches, cloth~s, housing and entertainment.

College graduates simply couldn't understand what I was objecting to.

Yuppies also couldn't understand why I objected to the idea that, in return for their salaries, professors owe us nothing but their self-righteousness.

Social science professors genuinely cannot understand the difference between crushing their right to free speech and refusing to pay for their lunch. So no matter how often this distinction is repeated, liberals go right back to the line that if the Internal Revenue Service does not force me to pay for some "Artist's" production of *The Intimate Commode* through the National Endowment for the Arts, then I am engaged in censorship.

Professors have the right to my money and there is no limit to the amount of government force that will be used to force me to provide it. Our established religion says that every professor has a right to get paid for any opinion he happens to want to push.

At this point I will be asked, "Bob, what do you

have in mind as an alternative to the present system? How can we pay professors to be accountable?"

Once again this question astonishes me. I am
supposed to come up with a system of accountability
for social scientists. I am also supposed to pay social
scientists to be full-time social experts and planners.

If I am paying them, why do I have to come up
with this new system? Why don't they do it?

But it would never occur to any college graduate
that perhaps the professors I am paying should have
to come up with a way for us to provide their lunches
and housing in an accountable way.

Maybe the social scientists, those self-righteous
people who tell young people how only they should
rule the world, could do a little real thinking for their
money.

The fact that it is the social scientists that should
come up with an accountable system in return for
their livelihood would simply never have occurred to
anybody if I hadn't brought it up!

The job of a liberal has always been to run interference for the professors. Any time anybody objects
to anything liberals do, liberal commentators throw
up roadblocks. They shout "academic freedom," they
shout, "Censorship!"

In other words, if anybody objects on basics, liberals go on the offensive.

Anybody who is experienced in debate knows
what to do if you have no case: You attack like hell.

This is an old tactic, and it scares off respectable
conservatives.

By the time a respectable conservative has finished defending himself against charges of censorship, Nazism, lack of compassion, anti-intellectualism, extremism, trouble-making, lack of sophistication, hatred, and bad breath, everybody has completely forgotten that it is the social scientists who

live at my expense, not the other way around.

If I pay you, it is your job to come up with a job description that makes it worth my money.

If you agree with me that social science professors have a natural set of biases, ANY biases, then social science has failed its most basic test. Exposing normal human biases happens to be exactly what social scientists get paid for.

Biases are a natural part of human motivation. You would expect that those we pay to study human motivations would look for their own biases first.

So you either 1) conclude that social scientists constitute the only profession on earth that has no human biases at all or 2) you face the fact that social science is not doing anything to earn its money.

Unless you conclude that social scientists constitute the only profession in human history with no biases, you must conclude that they are the last group with the right to claim "academic freedom."

Social scientists have never come up with any biases in their own profession. Social scientists will fight as hard as any business monopoly for the proposition that they cannot possibly abuse their own power.

So why do we call them "social scientists?" That is obviously the last thing that our so-called "intellectuals" are.

The Professors' Perfectly Tame "Young Revolutionaries"

No serious dissent is allowed on university campuses. But the words "dissent" and "revolution" and "rebellion" are used all the time.

Students who demand Marxism, that is, students who demand that professors should rule the world NOW, are called "revolutionaries." In the real world, nothing is less revolutionary on a college campus than what is called "dissent."

Many of these silly little "revolutionaries" are the thugs academia uses to enforce Political Correctness. When somebody like Arthur Jensen challenges leftist orthodoxy on campus, these "young revolutionaries" are the ones who riot and threaten them. This "potential for violence" is then used as an excuse to forbid all such real dissent.

These Storm Troopers of Political Correctness are called "student radicals." They demand that professors rule the world right now instead of later. By citing these so-called "revolutionaries," professors can call themselves moderates. This "young radicals" label given to the most obedient students on campus is a typical leftist strategy. It is the Big Lie with all the advantages the Big Lie gives those in power. It is such an absurdity you don't know where to start making fun of it.

Calling the enforcers of Political Correctness "young radicals" reminds me of an incident Aleksander Solzhenitsyn discussed in his Gulag Archipelago trilogy. In Stalin's Soviet Union there was a town meeting. The speaker ended a speech with a rousing tribute to Comrade Stalin. Needless to say, the crowd stood up and cheered and applauded.

They kept standing and they kept applauding for a few minutes. Then everyone came to a sudden realization: the first person to stop applauding Stalin's name would be arrested in the morning. They kept standing and clapping for five minutes, ten minutes.

After half an hour or so, someone sat down. He and the next person to sit down, sure enough, were arrested the next morning.

It was at this time and place, the Soviet Union in the 1930s, when one of the slogans used was "Have the courage to support Comrade Stalin." In other words, the official line was that it took real courage to back Stalin when every real person was terrified not to. This is exactly like today's media line that Marxists at universities are somehow "independent thinkers" and "revolutionaries" and "radicals" and represent some kind of dissent.

Like all oppressive regimes, Political Correctness uses the Big Lie. To call one of these perfectly obedient young Marxists a "radical" is exactly like calling a Russian supporter of Joseph Stalin in the 1930s "courageous." It is so ridiculous a lie that you don't know where to grasp it or how to begin to ridicule it.

That is the whole point of the Big Lie technique.

The so-called "campus radicals" are exactly as "rebellious" as Hitler's Storm Troopers were.

Professor-Priests Are Also Professor-Prophets

I am about the least conservative person in America. But I have to refer to myself as "conservative" and "on the right," because I am one of the many kinds of people who oppose the political left.

Anyone who does not think that professors should rule the world is labeled a "conservative."

Those very words show you that professors are looked upon as the prophets of our national religion.

Liberals refer to themselves as "progressives" and no one ever questions that title. But to be a progressive, you have to be a prophet. A progressive, by definition, is a person who is moving toward an inevitable future. That means that we take it for granted that liberals can predict the future.

You can only call yourself a "progressive" if you are moving toward the future. You can only move toward the future if you know what the future is. A person who can predict the future is a prophet.

It is not entirely accidental that when a professor-priest says he is a "progressive" and therefore a prophet, no one ever raises the slightest question. Professors are the only non-greedy people in our society, fit to judge the greed of all others and never to be asked about their own. Professors are the only dictators of culture in our society, whose job it is to dictate our True Multiculture.

Professors are the only people who can be trusted to dictate every phase of our lives.

What could be more natural than that our saintly professors should be our prophets, too?

On campus, any kind of leftist is looked upon as a prophet. "Progressive" is a term which covers the whole left, no matter how wrong its predictions are.

If we dump our established religion we can start using English again.

Got Pet Commies? Then Get Pet Nazis

Those perfectly tame "young Revolutionaries" are very useful to our leftist professor-priesthood. This is not a new phenomenon. Extremists have always been useful for the ruling group, whether it was a leftist ruling group or a rightist ruling group..

In the early 1920s a fairly typical article in a business magazine contained a sentence that sounds very strange today.

That sentence was,

"Not everything about the Italian fascists is good."

Huh?

Yep, that's what it said:

"Not everything about the fascists is good."

In 1917 Russia had just gone Communist. Lenin had instituted the Red Terror. Communist Parties were growing all over the world. The middle class was terrified. Businessmen were terrified.

Communism was new and frightening and there seemed to be no one to stop the Red Terror. When fascists hit the streets, their coming seemed providential to the frightened middle class.

There was a force of thugs on the streets to face down the Bolshevik thugs.

Businessmen were so happy to see those anti-Communist fascists hit the streets that they actually had to remind each other that not everything about the fascists was good.

Right-wing extremists are useful to the left on campus. Right-wing extremists were a godsend to conservatives in the 1920s. The right and extreme leftists are useful to professors on today's campuses for the same two reasons.

Today the fake "young revolutionaries" on campus give professors a chance to look moderate and reasonable.

But here is something else that right-wing extremists provided for the right in the 1920s. They shouted down radicals and yelled "Communist!" at them.

Leftist extremists on campus scream down all opposition to leftist orthodoxy. They sometimes use physical violence against all challenges to leftism.

Campus leftists are called Young Idealists when they use violence.

But there is another, more accurate word for people who use threats and fear.

They are called thugs.

Thugs

When I was young and snakes had feet, a professor named Schumpeter wrote a book called Communism, Socialism and Democracy. Back then, in the 1950s, labor unions were growing fast. Back then workers were assumed to be leftist politically.

"Communism, Socialism and Democracy" was dedicated to a discussion of what ideology would rule the world's future. Like all books by professors, then this one concluded that socialism would take over the world. When socialism took over, "intellectuals" would decide who worked where and who got money. This particular professor said socialism was inevitable because socialism had more thugs.

Naturally, the word "thugs" was not mentioned. What this particular socialist professor said was that, since the fall of fascism, workers were the more physical, threatening group. He said laborers would steadily scare the middle class into accepting socialism.

The only question, said this book, was whether the middle class would wait on labor thugs to impose Communism, or whether it would vote in democratic socialism.

In 1920 it was the Communists who owned the streets. The middle class did not know how to deal with the impending Workers' Revolution. They were ecstatic when the SS hit the streets in Germany against the Communists. They were happy when the Fascists took back the streets in Italy.

No, "not everything about the fascists is good." But for a terrified middle class in the 1920s they seemed like saviors.

And today, when professors want to encourage left wing extremism and crush right wingers, violent minorities and Marxist "young revolutionaries" are providential, God's gift to the "intellectuals."

There is no place in America for racism. But there is plenty of room for Marxism. Racism is Evil. Marxism is Healthy Dissent.

If professors are human, all this is completely predictable.

If professors are human, a campus is naturally a place where "There is no room for racism," but all the room in the world for Healthy Dissent.

Healthy Dissent means leftism. "Racism" means anything leftists don't like.

If professors are human, minority thugs are encouraged to cow the political right. Conservatives love to bitch about how white separatism is condemned on campus but black separatism is encouraged.

To a reasonably intelligent person it is obvious that professors will routinely condemn whites and encourage non-white resentment. A person with any moral courage at all would mention this.

The problem is that if you are a reasonably intelligent person with any courage at all you cannot be a respectable conservative.

Leftism depends heavily on white guilt, so if anyone questions white guilt liberal professors call out the thugs.

There is no money in black guilt. There is all the money in the world in white guilt. So if anyone questions white guilt, it is time to call out the Minority thugs to shut them up.

Minority and Marxist thugs are enormously useful for kicking rightist dissenters into line.

Professors encourage leftist thugs because professors are human and black thugs and "young revolutionary" thugs are useful to them.

So naturally all the respectable conservatives will leap up and shout "I'm against ALL thugs!" They make a big thing of condemning both the extreme left and the extreme right. That is the formula for being respectable.

This respectable conservative formula makes it sound like both rightist and leftist thugs are an equal problem on a real world campus. As usual with what respectable conservatives say, this is nonsense.

Meanwhile, back on Planet Earth, things are not that simple.

So let's take a quick look at the universities that exist down here on Planet Earth:

1) they are publicly supported, either directly by tax money or partially by tax deductions;

2) the institutional bias of all higher education is hard left.

In the real world, anything professors want to consider racist or rightist gets suppressed by them and their thugs as a matter of course.

They don't think they're being biased.

So you can't deal with this institutional bias if you just leave it up to the professors and respectable conservatives.

For ideological diversity on campus, you will need ideological affirmative action on campus.

Professors love to say that professors who get paid to openly demand genocide against whites like Noel Ignatiev represent "ideological diversity" and "intellectual courage." They say that the screaming thugs who call themselves Young Idealists on campus represent courageous thinking.

Respectable conservatives say that universities just to need to hire some respectable conservatives who are carefully selected by leftist faculties. No way. We need to crack the inbred university system wide open.

What we really must have is professors who are hated and denounced by today's university establishment. If there is room on campus for professors who call themselves Communists then there is room on campus for those others call racists.

A revolution today's professors approve of is not a revolution. We need the people professors HATE.

That is what a real revolution is all about.

What we call social science today is a fake.

Nothing that is not heresy can be social science. Period.

Do Young People Have To Be Dumb?

Neoconservatives like to say that "A young person who is not a socialist has no heart. An adult who is a socialist has no brain."

In other words, young people are supposed to be stupid.

I entered college at the age of sixteen, and it never even occurred to me to believe that an economy owned by the government and run by bureaucrats would be efficient. I was never a damned fool.

When I entered the university, all the Intellectuals believed that socialism was inevitable and that socialism was efficient. All the neoconservatives believed that, too, when they were young.

I don't have a high opinion of neoconservatives.

A lot of people who go to college believe what they are told. They are told that professors should rule the world and they are dumb enough to believe it. This is not Idealism, this is being mindless.

In other words, Johnny is a socialist because Johnny is not thinking. And until we get over the idea that there is something charming about being mindless on campus, Johnny is not going to learn to think.

Part Three
Only An Intellectual Revolution Can Create A Real Social Science

This is Not The First Time So-Called "Intellectuals" Have Gone Around The Bend

Universities have gone nuts before. This is not the first time in history our society has desperately needed to separate itself from an academia that has gotten so out of touch as to be actually insane.

My older brother — the every fifth child is Chinese brother — went to medical school when he was eighteen. Naturally I decided I would be a doctor too. Our house had lots of books on the history of medicine in it. Nothing could have been calculated to give me less blind faith in what the Learned University Doctors agreed on.

I found that when medicine was primitive, the Learned Doctors were not only always wrong, they were always DISASTROUSLY wrong. I later found that this is true at the primitive stage of any field of study.

Social scientists today freely admit that their fields of study are primitive compared to the hard sciences, and I have heard them discourse on this point at length. But it never occurs to any of them to mention the fact that all other primitive fields of study, like the social sciences today, always make unanimous recommendations that are not only consistently wrong, but disastrous.

The fact that historians have not mentioned this obvious fact shows that today's historian is the last person who can learn from history.

The doctors who bled George Washington to death to cure his pneumonia had plenty of experience. They had watched hundreds of patients weaken and die as their blood was let out of their veins.

But reality taught eighteenth century University Doctors nothing because they believed in the classical medicine of Galen. The Roman doctor Galen had had a preposterous theory that said, among other things, that you had to bleed patients to cure them of almost anything.

University professors today demand that child molesters be rehabilitated. When that doesn't work, they demand more money be spent on the rehabilitation of these basically sweet people, just as the old doctors insisted that, if taking a quart of blood didn't cure pneumonia, taking two quarts would.

Unfortunately, there is no solution to this situation if we maintain any respect at all for social science professors. The fact was that the doctors who were bleeding people with fever to death were WRONG. They would counter that they had long, long experience, so they knew best.

The University Doctors of 1799 would sneer at an outsider like me and everybody would agree with them. Who the hell did I think I was to say that they were being just plain silly?

And that, ladies and gentlemen, is exactly where the social sciences stand today.

And not just the social scientists themselves. Remember that people who have degrees and other people who are on university faculties resent anyone calling a major section of academia absurd. The stakes are enormous.

Ever since I entered college, I have been looked upon as an enemy within the gates. Now that people are beginning to understand how intolerant Political Correctness really is, readers may begin to understand that I paid for this dearly.

Not that long ago, it was taken for granted that liberals at universities were champions of Free Speech. In all the movies back then only the actors playing "reactionaries" would deny a fair hearing to the opposition.

Meanwhile, in the real world of the 1960s, those of us labeled "anti-intellectual" were not only suppressed fiercely, but nobody believed we were under any handicap at all.

Had I not read medical history in my teens I might have been able to go to college with the conviction that social scientists are wise in the ways of the world. Had I not read anti-intellectual heresy before entering college I might have agreed that only anti-intellectuals and fascists could ever think that today's professors are simply being absurd.

Things Are Not All That Bad

Our social policy is in the emergency room. We pay more and more money for worse and worse schools.

Most of our children will soon be born bastards. This latter fact is hardly noticed it is so much taken for granted. Drug addiction is taken as a given the way outbreaks of bubonic plague were back in the Middle Ages.

This book says that hope is on the way. This book says that our problem is not a Giant, Evil Conspiracy of all of Society's Great Minds. Our problem is a bunch of degree-holding yokels who get paid to tell each other and everybody else that they're "intellectuals."

Reading a conservative publication is like reading the Grave-Digger's Gazette. All the brilliant minds in our society are arrayed on the side of crazy ideas. That is the way respectable conservatives get paid to think

You can't be a respectable conservative if you don't take liberals seriously. You can't get on a talk show if you just laugh at the adults who never outgrew their college education.

But if you take leftism seriously, things do indeed look pretty hopeless.

I see leftism the same way I see the medicine of the year 1800. Back then if you were operated on or had a baby, the doctor would come straight from the dissecting room without washing his hands.

If you had any disease, the first thing your doctor would do would be to take a dirty knife and cut your veins and make you bleed a while. So, back then, if you had a medical problem things looked pretty hopeless.

Today our social problems look as bad as medical problems did in 1800.

If you do what the average patient did in 1800 and get under your bed in a fetal position, suck your thumb, and demand to see a priest, your condition will indeed be hopeless.

On the other hand, you could realize what the real situation is. Once medicine finally did that, an infection or a birth no longer had to be fatal.

But please note this absolutely critical point: as long as people took the same approach to nineteenth century medicine that conservatives do on social issues today, the patient was dead meat.

When the doctor comes in to treat you, it is absolutely critical that he wash his hands. He can read Plato and Aristophanes and Catholic Theology and not wash his hands, and you're still dead meat.

If you have a fever and you don't want to die, the doctor has to have some of those penicillin spores. You and he can talk seriously about the Philosophy of Medicine and you can admire his MD and you two can reason together at public expense, but in the end you either get the spores or you die.

So how much hope was there when you went into a doctor's office in 1850?

The answer to that question depended entirely on how much you dealt with washing hands and getting spores.

How much hope is there in dealing with today's social problems?

It depends entirely on how much you deal with real solutions and not the leftist's favorite Social Questions.

To me, every single Respectable Conservative Spokesman is a roadblock. Conservative publications are certainly right about their gloom. As long as you depend on reading Thucydides or theology or Deep Thoughts shared with liberals to take care of anything, you can kiss the patient goodbye.

But each time we look at the disease for what it is, we see the bacteria and the poisons in the system. AND NOTHING ELSE.

Once we start demanding that social policies WORK, and nothing else, then we are on our way to making them WORK, and nothing else.

Make the professors wash their hands, and the disease will reverse itself drastically.

Get rid of the professors who teach that they do not need to wash their hands, and you can stop the plague at its source.

Modern conservatism is chicken soup. There is a very specific problem. If you deal with that problem you will cure the disease. Every minute you focus on anything but the runaway infection we face, you are killing the patient.

You know the old joke, a boy is sick and his Jewish mother offers him chicken soup.

"Will it help?," he asks hoarsely.

"Well, says his mother, "It can't hurt."

In this case nobody knows what to do and the soup is comforting, so it can't hurt.

But if anyone actually thinks the chicken soup is a substitute for getting to the real cause of the disease it can kill.

So calling modern Conservatism chicken soup may sound like a joke. But when it kills, there is nothing funny about it.

Today it is hilarious to read about the hideous concoctions prescribed by doctors in the old days, from poultices of dung to crushed pearls. But there was nothing funny about the despair of the people who were subjected to these things instead of cures.

But we are still arguing over pearl dust and manure.

The nostrums of social scientists are already being laughed at. "It's all Society's fault" is so absurd it was a Monty Python line a generation ago.

When half of the political debate is silly, the opposition can be nothing but ridiculous, too.

The pompous pretensions and theocratic nonsense preached by National Review and the like are exactly what you would expect in this situation. They are a group of clichés rattled off to face a group of leftist clichés.

We need a serious social science. Developing some real social science after all this wasted time will be a titanic challenge that will never be complete

Developing modern medicine since 1800 has been a very titanic challenge that will never be complete. But to begin it we first had to toss Galen and bleeding and University Medicine and insect dung mixers and powdered pearls into the garbage dump.

To get rid of bleeding was not an intellectual challenge. It was a moral decision that took moral courage. To stop talking about Humors and get University doctors to wash their hands required moral courage, not high intellect.

Modern medicine began with the decision to stop sounding good and start saving lives.

Modern medicine began with the unshakable decision that medicine had to WORK.

Modern social science will start when their programs have to WORK.

Modern social science will begin when we have to state a goal and reach it. Once modern social science begins you will have to say what you want and prove you can do it.

Say what you want and prove you can do it. That is what every adult is expected to do about every serious question.

This entire book is dedicated to the simple proposition that if we pay professors, professors should be forced to get serious.

If you look at today's situation in these historical terms, things are not at all hopeless. The time will come when we can look back at the nostrums of today's social science and college graduates who are still mental six-year-olds the way we laugh at prescriptions from the year 1800.

With luck, we will soon be able to laugh at leftism (and its rightist shadow) the way we laugh at the medicine that killed George Washington.

Semmelweis Solutions

Doctor Ignac Semmelweis was one of many martyrs to science who found that what sounds good is far more important to primitive "experts" than the truth.

Puerperal Disease, or "childbed fever," killed hundreds of millions of women and children over the weary millennia. All the Medical Intellectuals said puerperal fever came from Imbalanced Humors or (yes, it was popular centuries ago) from Deep Seated Psychosomatic Causes.

In 1848, a young doctor named Semmelweis found that childbed fever could be stopped if the Great Medical Experts would simply wash their hands before delivering babies. It was the least salable explanation imaginable. It was too simple, too obvious. So, for a generation, millions of women and babies died in agony because the Medical Authorities were unanimously against Semmelweis.

The same thing happened with vaccinations.

The same thing happened with the bacterial theory of disease. Millions died while Medical Authority and Intellectuals fought for the Humor Theory of Disease, for which there was no evidence except the fact that Authority supported it.

Like political leftism, the Humor Theory of Disease never worked, but university "intellectuals" in primitive medicine unanimously supported it.

One after another, each one of these common sense Semmelweis Solutions had to be sold over the screams of the Authorities and Intellectuals while millions died.

Medicine only began to be a science when it discredited all the old Intellectuals. A field of study can only be a science when it decides that if you have a cure that WORKS on one side and all the Intellectuals and Authorities on the other, Authority means nothing.

Semmelweis saved a few thousand lives personally. He has saved millions since, and he is saving them right now.

But in his lifetime, this forgotten hero of humanity watched millions die while he wore himself out trying to point out the simple reality that would save them.

Because he loved humanity too much for his own good, Semmelweis died in a madhouse.

Servetus Solutions

Those who do not want Semmelweis Solutions tell us that we should not be extremists. We must not go after the priesthood of social science with hammer and tong. The truth, they tell us, lies somewhere in the middle of the road, in moderation

There is a charming little story about the sixteenth century preacher Michael Servetus. It was in the period when Catholics killed Protestants and Protestants killed Catholics in massive religious wars.

One of the most fanatical of anti-Catholics was John Calvin, who ruled the Swiss city of Geneva. It was a very unusual case when he and the Pope cooperated on anything, but they did cooperate in prosecuting Michael Servetus. Servetus was a Unitarian. Calvin arrested Servetus for heresy, and for once Calvin and the Catholics cooperated.

The Catholic authorities sent evidence to Calvin to convict Servetus.

The result? Well, that's where the charming quote comes in:

"Servetus began to scream when the flames reached his face. He kept screaming for over twenty minutes."

I like to think of this charming little scene as the direct result of Moderation in action. It was, you know. Moderates tell us that truth is always somewhere in the middle of the road. Servetus was a Unitarian so he was not between Catholics and Protestants.

When Catholics and Protestants acted in brotherly cooperation against Servetus, it was a triumph of the idea that "The truth lies in the middle of the road."

"The truth lies somewhere in the middle" is unmitigated horseshit when it comes to science, including a real social science.

In American politics, the one thing you can say to sound wise is that "to get elected, one must go to the middle of the road." But even here, if you look at the voting records of congressmen who actually get elected, that pure manure goes right out the window. Real elected officials are either left or right.

But "the Middle Way," Moderation, and "both sides have a point" just sounds so wise it hypnotizes everybody.

When there are crises in a society, Moderation is the best way to make it worse. In a time when an established religion is warping and destroying a society, we must face the ruling theocracy head on. That is the time when moderation is a Servetus Solution, a recipe for horror.

In the Middle Ages anyone who saw the universe through a telescope had to adjust his findings to suit the Bible. Now every genetic study has to explain itself in terms of Political Correctness.

And you know something? Every single Medieval professor was a person who found a Biblical explanation for everything he reported.

And you know something else? Every single science professor and every geneticist who wants to work on grant money finds a Politically Correct explanation for every discovery he reports.

When the Human Genome Project was proposed, many social scientists were upset at the idea of putting so much money into a study of human genetics. They feared such a study would upset the present Scientific Balance.

The old Scientific Balance was to say that there was no heredity because Hitler believed in it. The new balance is to say that human action is partly the result of environment and partly of heredity, and then ignore heredity totally.

Professors can mention heredity and then ignore it because nobody on campus is ever going to ask about heredity in a social science class.

But even college students have some limits to their credulity. Social scientists were concerned that if you had a huge study on human genetics like the Human Genome Project even some college graduates could come out of their hypnotic trance.

In order to prevent social science faculties from vetoing human genetics studies of any kind, geneticists must be the first to absolutely guarantee their perfect orthodoxy in the faith of Political Correctness.

The proposal for the Human Genome Project was based on a study by three scientists, all of whom had absolutely guaranteed their own orthodoxy. One of them gave his entire prize to the Black Panthers.

The required line on Political Correctness today is that there is no such thing as race.

Almost all the Olympic sprint races are won by blacks from one side of Africa and all the long-distance ones are won by people from the opposite corner of black Africa.

You cannot get a job as a forensic pathologist if you are unable to tell the age, sex AND RACE of an unrecognizable corpse.

You cannot be a physical anthropologist if you cannot tell someone's racial origin, preferably from blood studies alone.

And you cannot teach any of these subjects on a university campus unless you line up and swear that there is no such thing as race.

The Human Genome Project got funded only after everybody in it swore it would conclude that race does not exist. Political Correctness wants for race not to exist, so you can get a thousand professors in any field you want to line up and sign a statement that race does not exist.

Respectable conservatives say the truth lies somewhere in the middle.

As always, university science is solidly behind the established religion. Anything social science wants to be true is confirmed immediately by any genetics professor who wants a promotion or a mainline research grant.

In an Inquisition, no department creates problems for the School of Theology. Communists called their College of Theology Marxist Studies. The Nazis called their Theology School Racial Studies. We call our School of Theology the Social Sciences.

But the moment any Inquisition ends, EVERY real advance creates nightmares for the Theology Department. Heresy has been avoided for so long that all the discoveries and advances that have piled up and been ignored during the Inquisition are going to involve heresy.

There is no moderate way to deal with an Inquisition. Today nothing that is not heresy can be serious social science.

Only in a primitive field is the truth a matter of compromise. You can't say anything really radical so the way you get a doctoral degree, tenure and promotion is to find out where everybody else is and fit in.

But you cannot advance science without being intolerant of anything that doesn't yield results. As in all primitive fields of study, the one thing we know for sure about social science, which admits it is primitive, is that the truth does NOT lie in the middle of the road it has so far established.

That much is for sure. As in the case of Semmelweis and the germ theory of disease, all advances will require pure heresy because the cry of "Heresy" is what keeps everything blocked up.

In order for astronomy to begin to be a real science, we did not need another expert on proving that the Bible was right and the earth was the center of the universe. Every professor could do that.

We don't need any more fake revolutionaries to demand that professors should rule the world.

We do not need more students of Marxism or Maoism or the Criminal as a Victim of Society. We must fire all the standard social science professors just as you needed to get rid of every university expert on the Humor Theory of Galen.

To keep his job, every university professor of medicine had to backtrack hard and fast or just retire. That is the formula for social science today.

The Redneck Theory Of Disease

I call the germ theory of disease a "redneck" theory because that was exactly the way it was regarded through most of medical history.

There was always a bunch of uneducated people who noticed that when you bled a person he got weaker. University Doctors pitied these people because they could not understand the Humor Theory of Disease.

Uneducated people of this sort just saw that bleeding didn't work. They did not have the education and sophistication to Understand True Medicine.

People who saw animals from elephants to gnats could imagine that even tinier beings might exist and cause disease. Such people were forgiven for their ignorance, though True Intellectuals did sometimes get frustrated with them.

Actually, the germ theory of disease had been proposed over and over and over throughout Western European history. The Medical Intellectuals laughed at the germ theory. They pointed to Galen and to the fact that Galen could only be read in the Intellectuals' Language, Latin.

Sounds a lot like social science professors today, doesn't it?

We are all aware that syphilis is a bacteriological disease, produced by a bacterium, a tiny, tiny organism that is found in the blood stream. We kill it with antibiotics.

When syphilis broke out in Europe in the sixteenth century, university-trained medical experts had to deal, once again, with the usual bunch of non-university Germans who said syphilis, like other diseases, came from tiny organisms in the blood stream, i.e., germs.

John Astruc, physician to Louis XIV, set out to get rid of this germ theory nonsense once and for all. You can almost hear him drawing in a long, frustrated breath at once again having to deal with this nonsense, much like a social scientist today would sigh at having to deal with a critic of Progressive Social Policy.

Says Astruc, "There are some, however, whom I forebear now to spend time in imputing, such as Augustus Hauptman and Christian Langius, who think that the venereal disease is nothing else but a numerous school of nimble, brisk, invisible living things, of a very prolific nature, which when once admitted, increase and multiply in abundance; which lead frequent colonies to different parts of the body and inflame, erode and exulcerate the parts they fix on....."

"In short, which without regard to the particular quality of any humor occasion all the symptoms that occur in venereal disease. But as these are mere visionary imaginations, UNSUPPORTED BY ANY AUTHORITY, they do not require any argument to refute them..."

Here we have the entire weight of what we today call Progressive Opinion. Everything Astruc says is very familiar.

Also familiar to those used to dealing with today's admittedly primitive social science is the next part of John Astruc's condemnation of the bacteriological theory of disease. He said that heresy would lead to more heresy:

Astruc said that if you accepted the germ theory of syphilis, the entire science of medicine could be destroyed. This is what he said:

"If it was once admitted that the venereal disease

could be produced by invisible living things swimming in the blood, one might with equal reason allege the same thing, not only of plague, as Athanasius Kircher, the Jesuit, and John Saguens, a Minim, lately have done. (Germs could also be said to cause) hydrophobia, itch, tetters and other contagious diseases, and indeed all the distempers whatsoever; and thus the whole Theory of Medicine would fall to the ground, as nothing could be said to prove the venereal disease depending upon little living things which might not be urged to prove that all other diseases were derived from the like little living things though of a different species, THAN WHICH NOTHING COULD BE MORE RIDICULOUS."

If you admit one heresy, there will be more heresy. So Astruc said he could not allow any medical heresy to be spoken.

Today, any challenge to Progressive Thought is crushed by using Political Correctness. The ultimate argument used by today's university social science faculty is that if you accept heresy on one issue, you will accept heresy on all of them.

Any recognition that genes might influence human history leads straight into Nazism!

Before anybody even hints that it is an exaggeration to say that today's social science says that any heresy leads to Nazism, let me give you a quick example, one of many.

There are two general theories of human evolution. One says modern man originated in Africa. The other says there was a "parallel development" on different continents. But anybody who says "parallel development" can be immediately accused of being racist.

In one of the denials of this charge, the main exponent of parallel development today said, "We all know that human evolution has nothing to do with human society. We have seen where the idea that human evolution affects human society in the acts of Adolph Hitler."

Let me remind you that not one single person was puzzled for a split second as to why a supposed scientist had to call up Hitler to witness his ideological purity.

But let me ask you this, what if a geneticist were to say that, "We all know where a purely social theory of society leads directly to the historical actions of Joseph Stalin." I dare say that that man would never find a job again at any university.

In the first place, practically nobody would know what the hell he was talking about. In the second place, a small number of social scientists would know exactly what he was talking about, and they would ruin anybody who said that.

So now back to John Astruc, the physician to Louis XIV, who was once again condemning the redneck germ theory of syphilis in the name of all university intellectual medicine. Astruc first pointed out that this provincial and silly and unprogressive germ nonsense was rejected by all Authorities, and therefore did not need to be argued against.

Astruc sounded exactly like today's trendy leftists. All the professors, Asruc said, were on his side.

What Astruc said was that if bacteria were really the cause of syphilis, then the whole theory of medicine, Galen's Theory of Humors that all medical professors accepted, would have to be abandoned.

He was right.

All those diseases WERE caused by those little living things of a different species, and for that reason the whole theory of medicine had to fall to the ground before it could save human life and stop killing people.

And that is the message of this book. We cannot

have a social science until the whole present theory of social science falls to the ground.

Liberal media choose who will be allowed to speak for the opposition. These are the respectable conservatives, given that label by the media. Naturally, they are those who are in respectful and "reasonable" disagreement with others who graduated from college and share the ideas their professors inculcated in them.

Since an intellectual revolution is demanded, these respectable conservatives have no more place in the next age than today's social scientists do. In fact, they make revolution more difficult because their approach sounds so rational.

But the left is not merely partially mistaken; it is a predictably dangerous, out-of-control bundle of pure nonsense that simply boils down to "Professors should rule the world."

It cannot be dealt with by respectful disagreement, any more than astrology could be turned into astronomy or Galen's Humor Theory could be turned into real medicine by small stages.

Today's social science is as stupid and as outdated as Galen's Theory of Medicine, and until that fact is recognized it will remain as deadly as the Humor Theory was.

Another Quick Review: If You See That The Emperor Has No Clothes, You Are "Simplistic"

In his book, "1984," George Orwell sums up his entire message this way: "Freedom is the right to say that 2 plus 2 equals 4."

The reason Orwell's statement is so wise is because propagandists always try to tell us that things are not as they appear.

Your professor told you that all the things he said are really very, very complex. But what one learns from a lifetime of experience is that people's real motivations, no matter how many degrees they have, are very simple. Any human being who is hired to talk daily for years to a captive audience will do what any human being does when he talks: he tries to look good.

All humans, left to their own devices, say whatever they think makes them look good. No matter how hard I try, WhitakerOnline.org is going to contain lots of references to my background and my experience, and not all of them are going to be for your benefit.

Benjamin Franklin's short autobiography is great because he starts off by admitting that the main reason he wrote about himself was his own ego.

But almost every European or Canadian will look you straight in the eye and tell you that his teachers and professors did not push political leftism and socialism because political leftism and socialism makes professors look good.

This simple fact has never occurred to anybody, though if you think about it just a moment you will realize it is one of the most important facts in the world today.

Like supply and demand, once you actually look at professor's natural human biases, it changes your whole view of the world. What is terribly hard is to get people to see how important this simple fact is.

No matter how "complex" and "unsimplistic" you get, you can't know anything about real world economics until you have done a lot of thinking about supply and demand.

By the same token, you are simply not IN this world until you have done some serious thinking about the UNAVOIDABLE human biases of the people who ruled your life for the eight years of high school and college.

To repeat:

It is not surprising that almost all Europeans and Canadians worship professors. It is a tribute to Americans that so many Americans went through eight years of this and it didn't take.

What if every child were required to spend eight years in military school? What if those same kids ended up being militarists and fascists? The connection would seem a bit obvious, right?

So our teachers, who call themselves "Intellectuals," tell us how a Truly Just Society is to be run. Here are some predictable things they say:

Businessmen are Evil. What we need to do is to turn economics over to the Planners and the professors. This never works, but kids keep marching for it, especially at European universities. Has it ever occurred to anybody that for a university student to be a socialist is as inevitable as it would be for an entire generation sent to military school to be militarists?

So we have younger generations that have the terminal sillies. They insist that criminals are really nice people who have been perverted by Society. What we need, they say, is huge Rehabilitation programs planned by Criminologists. And the Europeans are still on the streets demanding this as their crime rate climbs out of sight.

Once you start thinking in these terms, it is as revealing as suddenly finding out about supply and demand. Everything we call "leftist" is simply what college professors would professionally prefer.

And notice that every school child knows all about the biases of military men, businessmen, doctors, and every other profession. But never once does anybody point out that teachers -- and your teachers' professors -- have just as many biases that are just as natural.

Have you ever heard anybody in the national media even MENTION this possibility?

If You See The Emperor Has No Clothes You Are Anti-Intellectual

Every occupation has a label for people who criticize that occupation.

In 1903, the owners of Big Steel would sit around a table and set steel prices nationwide. They did this in the name of Private Enterprise. Anybody who criticized price fixing was called an enemy of Private Enterprise, a Socialist.

Obviously the whole purpose of price fixing is to get rid of private enterprise. So in 1903 the ruling group used the label "Private Enterprise" as an excuse to fight private enterprise.

If you consider this an exception to the rule, you do not understand how the world works. Anybody who wants to control and limit the field they are in does so in the name of advancing the field they are in. A reader may think it is ironic that the Semmelweis cure was blocked in the name of Medical Science.

It was not ironic, it was routine.

The fight against our academic tyranny is met with the charge that it is "anti-intellectual." What we are trying to do is to open a suffocating academia to fresh air and new ideas. But New Ideas are exactly what Professors, and Political Correctness, insist that they – and ONLY they – represent.

Anybody who criticizes our inbred professorial bureaucracy is labeled an "anti-intellectual."

For anyone who understands how the real world works, this is not surprising. In the world it is inevitable that those who suppress real intellectualism will do so in the name of True Intellectualism.

We said that every occupation has labels it uses to defend itself from regulation. Nobody in the media ever mentions that "anti-intellectualism" is a label to prevent fresh air in the academic community.

Now comes a critical point. What we are discussing here is labels, not arguments.

A label is a completely different thing from an argument. An argument is used to convince people you are right. A label is thrown at somebody to keep them from mentioning the possibility you could be wrong.

A label is used to scare off opposition. As long as the only people who are allowed to oppose the left are terrified of your favorite labels, your power is absolute.

It is hard for a person who can take criticism to become really nasty or truly mean. It is the people who cannot imagine that they are anything but wonderful who get small and nasty.

If you can look at yourself from the outside there is a limit to how bad you can get. If you assume you are practically perfect in every way there is no limit to how bad you can get.

In other words, professors can go around the bend and stay around the bend as long as they have the right so-called "opposition." If their only critics are afraid of being called "anti-intellectual" or "simplistic" or even "racist," any serious criticism can be stopped before it starts.

American campuses are run by nasty little people who cannot imagine they can be wrong. They call themselves "intellectuals" and they call their thugs "idealists." In every way they are the exact opposite of what they claim to be.

This is not ironic, this is routine. Academia uses the word "diversity" to justify crushing all serious differences of opinion. This is not ironic, this is routine.

When the words of freedom are used to destroy

freedom, it is time for revolution, and nothing less than a revolution.

East Really Is East; West Really Is West

All of society's progress, the progress that saves lives and the progress that makes life worth living, depends on intellectual revolution.

In the history of medicine Semmelweis represented knowledge. Against Semmelweis was ranged the entire weight of Medical Wisdom.

In the history of medicine the germ theory represented a piece of knowledge. Ranged against the germ theory was the entire weight of Classical Wisdom, the Authority of Galen.

This is the history of Western science. In every primitive science we have an enormous accumulation of Authority behind things that simply do not work. But in the West, experience overthrows Authority. In other societies, priests or Wise men stay there and society stagnates.

Calling everybody from the Middle East to Japan by the name "The Orient" is now Politically Incorrect.

But like everything that is Politically Incorrect, there is a good reason for doing it.

One thing the Orient has in common is that Authority wins in the end. In Egypt, the priests of Amon were supplanted by the Imams. But they are still the same thing. Simple truth, things that actually work, lost out against Wisdom and Authority in Egypt and Mesopotamia.

In China, the Tao and other Chinese philosophies were supplanted by Marxist ideologues. But nothing really changed from a Western point of view. In China and in India Authority and Wisdom, Brahmans and Marxists, won over truths that worked, knowledge that was simply the truth, not the Final Truth.

So the entire Orient eventually stagnated. If the West ever adopts a priesthood completely, we too will stagnate as others have. But our present social science priesthood will not last because at least a part of the West will always remain rebellious.

When southern Europe stagnated, Northern Europe took up the challenge. While Europe is happy under its Politically Correct priesthood, middle America remains rebellious. And rebellious, as it produces results, becomes contagious.

Western culture conquered the East because the East stagnated. American culture conquers Europe where European culture stagnates.

Reality has no respect at all for priests and professors and Marxist ideologues. The only thing that can move the real world is knowledge.

As science progressed in the West during the late nineteenth century we came to look at the whole world that stagnated as a single Orient, despite the fact that this includes wildly different societies like India and China and the world of Islam.

This is looked upon by historians as simple Western provincialism. Westerners, said the sophisticates, were too ignorant to see the big differences between Arabia and Persia and India and China.

But when the West began to look on the Orient as a single unit, what we called the Orient had one thing in common: stagnation.

That general Oriental stagnation was what Kipling had in mind when he said the East was the East and the West was the West.

From a purely humanitarian point of view Oriental stagnation is more important than all the Chinese philosophers and Brahman Mystics and Islamic Imams that ever lived or will ever live.

And what is important to humans is important to me. Like businessmen and military men and Medieval priests, I am just a human being. And, may the gods of Political Correctness forgive me, I say professors are just human beings, too.

For mere human beings, "Do unto others as you would have them do unto you" is a better commandment than any philosophy or any Authority or any Wisdom that has ever existed.

Knowledge Versus Wisdom

In Ancient Egypt the Pharoah used to get up every morning to make sure that the sun would rise.

The ruling priests of Amon said that if the Pharoah didn't go through his morning ritual, the sun might stay down.

Other "Great Civilizations" based their power on the same thing. In Mesoamerica, Indian priests had to do their thing if the world was to continue to operate. People believed them.

After all, the priests were the teachers. Who was going to disagree with them?

Ancient Egypt's permanent and runaway best seller was "The Book of the Dead." It gave you detailed instructions about what to do as soon as you went permanently out of contact with the rest of the world.

Only the priests could tell you what would happen after you died. And there was no one to contradict them.

Western civilization is based on the exact opposite of what ancient priesthoods and modern social science is based on. The basis of Western science is called "the testable hypothesis."

In plain English, science is based on the idea that if it works, we can use it.

Please notice I did not say that western science says that something that works is the Truth. All we say is that if it works, it works. As you approach the speed of light Newtonian physics stops working. But in the world we live in Newtonian physics does very well because light speed is not our problem.

I think one of the foundations of Western science

lies in the Story of Woden the Father God of the Germanic and Scandinavian old religion. It is a very subtle thing, but it is critical.

Odin or Woden was a one-eyed god. He had given one eye for knowledge. Please understand that no one gets this right.   Wagner said that Odin gave one eye for love of his wife, the Goddess Freya. Numerous other sources will tell you that Woden gave his eye for Wisdom.

The truth is more subtle. The truth is more important.

In English we have a word for knowledge and a separate word for wisdom. In German we have Kennis and Weisheit. There are totally separate words for knowledge and wisdom in every Indo-European language. They mean different things, and the difference is very important.

Old Norse is the language in which the story of Odin was written. The story of Woden is told in each of the Germanic languages.

And every one of those languages had a word for "Wisdom" and a word for "Knowledge."

In every one of those languages, Woden gave an eye for knowledge, not for wisdom.

I have never heard of any other religion that claimed to be based on knowledge. They all claim that Wisdom, with the capital letter, is everything.

Odin wanted to know things. He hung on the world tree and lost an eye to know things. I think that is where the mentality that underlies Western thinking comes from.

Wisdom is a thing of priests and professors. All the Wisdom in the world will not cure a case of pneumonia or childbed fever or get the worms out of the gut of a hundred million Asian children.

Every Pharoah who made the sun come up in the morning had worms in his gut. Every Egyptian

High Priest who helped make the Nile flow at the right time of year had serious and often fatal vitamin deficiencies.

Priests And Professors Through History

So Western science developed slowly and painfully out of mere knowledge and simple truth. Oriental society developed Wisdom while the Pharoah and Mesoamerican priests ordered the sun to rise each day.

On the plus side, the Egyptian sun did come up every morning. On the minus side, the history of every Ancient Civilization, from Mesoamerica to the Middle East and China and India, quickly degenerated into a succession of priests and Imams and Karl Marx "Revolutionaries" like Mao Tse Tung, who was just an economic priest with fangs.

The parallels between Ancient Oriental Wisdom and today's social science are striking. In the Tao of China and in the Hinduism of Brahman India priests imposed the idea that the life of a mouse was as important as the life of a human. This concept of animal equality is now the basis of well-funded groups like Green Peace and People for the Ethical Treatment of Animals.

There's a branch on every campus.

I have a theory of how this sort of thing develops. Those who make their livings being priests or professors never do anything that WORKS in the real world. So they change the subject.

If nothing you do works, you can keep your following if you preach about Man's Guilt. Academics used to demand that "Intellectuals" rule every phase of society in the name of Karl Marx's Scientific Socialism.

The instant Karl Marx's Scientific Socialism was finally recognized as a laughable horror, the environmentalist movement demanded that professors rule the world in the name of animal life.

To a person who went to college and never grew out of it, the instant transition from socialism to environmentalism represents New Thinking.

To someone like me who has spent decades in the fight for power in Washington, the switch from socialism to environmentalism is business as usual.

Part Four
The Fake Opposition Must Go!

If You Want To Be A "Conservative Spokesman" You'd Better Not Bark, Either

Without big blocks of money there would be no political left in America. Professors live on tax money and captured foundation money. Leftist organizations live on money in big chunks.

On the left, Marxists talk about how they love the working class. But in a Marxist state no worker is allowed to say a thing. The "intellectuals" want a state where they rule and any worker who tries to escape gets shot.

Leftists always talk about their grassroots appeal, but they live only on big-money contributions.

So when liberals refer to the power of groups like the National Rifle Association (NRA), they think all that power comes from big money and nothing else, like liberal power does. If anybody ever explained the difference between the NRA and liberal groups, it would make a crushing, critical point.

No one ever does that.

When anti-gun liberals in the media talk about the power of the NRA, no one ever mentions that the National Rifle Association has over three million purely voluntary members. Each member pays substantial annual dues. Three million paid up, politically militant members would make any organization a major power.

I say "would make" because no other organization has three million paid-up voluntary grass-roots members.

No one makes any distinction between the one-of-a-kind NRA and all the groups in Washington which are financed by big money.

The only lobby in Washington that compares in

sheer power to the NRA is the Trial Lawyers' Association. Trial lawyers are the exact opposite of grassroots volunteers. The members of the Trial Lawyer's Association make their livelihoods in the law, and legislation is their bread and butter.

Grassroots NRA members do not make money on their political stance. Gun shop owners and gun collection owners tend to belong to the NRA. It is interesting to note that the one thing that is sure to cause a rise in the price of firearms is a threat of gun control legislation.

It is a horrible pun, but the National Rifle Association is a smoking gun in American politics.

The NRA's base is real working people.

After all, the National Rifle Association offers no general program for the right in the way that professors offer leftist programs where "intellectuals" would rule the world.

Leftist professors say they love The Working Class so much they want to take over the government and tell workers what to do. They even shoot workers who try to escape, they love them so much. A large part of the European working class fell for that crap and voted Communist.

You would have to look hard to find a single American worker who is dumb enough to be a Red.

In America only college students are stupid enough to take this Working Class bilge from professors seriously.

In Europe, professors rule the intellectual roost. In America, professors rule big money foundations and get big business money, but the grassroots knows who the enemy is.

In America, the left is financed by big money. In America it is the anti-left that is paid for by huge numbers of small donations. So the media say liberals have grassroots money and the right is financed by Big Business.

What is true of the NRA is true of other anti-liberal forces in Washington. By far the largest grassroots women's organizations are on the political right. They do not have anything like the funding that the National Organization for Women (NOW) disposes of, but NOW gets almost none of its power or its money from any grassroots membership.

NOW has power because editors want to print anything NOW says.

In order to be news you have to be news that a reporter can sell. If the media could sell stories on media scandals or foundation scandals there would be a supply of such stories. But a dog that barks at the left cannot sell.

For the same reason, the right doesn't bark about scandals on the left either.

In order to sell himself, a conservative "spokesman" must fit into the news world as it exists.

Listen closely when someone in the media asks whether anyone in Hollywood might discriminate against someone on the political right. Every conservative on a talk show will say Hollywood may be biased to the left, but there is no discrimination against the right in Hollywood.

Listen closely when someone in the media asks whether there could be any media scandals involving the kind of ideological evil Watergate represented. No, says every conservative spokesman, media owners are hard left, but every single one of them is an honest man, a fair man.

No one who is a recognized national spokesman for the right ever says that big-money leftists ever cheat. They say Ted Turner is a good man, an honest man, one who supports his convictions with an admirable idealism that everyone who gets to be a conservative spokesman admires loudly.

Even Rush Limbaugh says, "There will always be liberals." Liberals are legit. Liberals are honest. We may disagree with them, but they are truly fine, upstanding pillars of the community.

Nobody who fails to say that regularly becomes a Conservative Spokesman.

So every national spokesman tells us that the national takeover of the local press by national syndicates is a Historic First. For the first time in history a national industrial takeover is occurring without a breath of scandal, without a hint of dishonesty.

There used to be hundreds of separately owned local newspapers in America. These small businesses had a general bias to the political right. In every city these local newspapers are being taken over by national chains, all of which have a left bias.

If oil companies were taking over local monopolies in gas stations, one would expect some undue pressure, a little greed, maybe even a hint of outright viciousness in this coast-to-coast process.

In the national media takeover there has not been a hint of scandal. Conservative spokesmen are as desperate as liberal spokesmen to insist that every single big money man in the national media and the national entertainment industry is one hundred percent fair.

Respectable Conservatives: The Kept "Opposition"

The commentators you see on television and read in the syndicated columns are selected by a bureaucracy. Bureaucracies always choose people who "fit in."

Liberals run the media bureaucracy, and they only want to talk to conservatives they feel comfortable with.

This is why conspiracy theories sound so plausible. In the real world routine bureaucracy ACTS like a conspiracy. It seems planned, but it is actually quite mindless.

Routine bureaucracy acts like a conspiracy, but bureaucracy is not a conspiracy. A conspiracy is run from the top. You can remove any big man in the media bureaucracy and the body will act exactly the same.

When I refer to the "media bureaucracy" I am not using "bureaucracy" in the sense of a single organization of bureaucrats run from top to bottom.

The "media bureaucracy" simply means those who produce our media commentary. They all answer to each other, argue with each other, and select each other, so they constitute what amounts to a single bureaucracy.

For example, William Buckley became a champion media bureaucrat, though he never worked directly under anyone designated as the Chief of the Media Bureaucracy.

Buckley was selected for his role because he "fit" into the media bureaucracy. He became the perfect respectable conservative who would show just the right combination of criticism and respect for liberals.

So Buckley was chosen as a "respectable conservative" spokesman.

The obvious question here is: who is NOT part of the media bureaucracy?

Well, to start with, Matt Drudge is not a media bureaucrat. He selected himself, and the media bureaucracy hates him bitterly for it. As long as he succeeds by going directly to the market the way he does, he will not be declared "respectable." Any right-winger who has not gotten this "respectable" title from liberals is blocked from the mainline media.

If you are not a right-wing Uncle Tom, you are not allowed to open your mouth. Meanwhile, the Uncle Toms themselves are going to make sure those who refuse to be Uncle Toms are kept in their place. As you would expect, nobody is more fanatical in shouting down "right wing extremists" than respectable conservatives themselves. You can count on Jack Kemp or Orrin Hatch or William Bennett to jump right in on the attack on anyone the media call "racist." The Bushes and the Doles are at the head of any liberal lynch mob.

Bless his soul, Jeffrey Hart reviewed my book, A Plague on Both Your Houses, in 1976, in National Review under the title, "Read This One!" In this review he freely admitted that even people like him had to make truly bad concessions to liberals in order to get their case to the public through the media.

But Jeffrey Hart never became a full-fledged respectable conservative. He is allowed media access, but he will never be "one of the boys" like Bob Novak or William Buckley.

A conservative respectable will not hang onto real world truths that are uncomfortable for liberals, and he can be sidetracked very easily. You can count on Novak to be an economic theologue, and, in the end,

you can count on even Pat Buchanan to end up looking like a harmless religious nut.

While rewriting this, I was watching MSNBC. A
conservative laughed at a liberal who was giving the
same old routine spin. The liberal was terribly upset.
I have noticed this many times - when he is going
through his routine silliness and a rightist LAUGHS,
the liberal commentator gets terribly upset. Watch
and you will notice this, too. In the end it will be
LAUGHTER that will destroy our established religion.

The left will only be destroyed when people start
calling their nonsense "Nonsense!," and denounce
those who keep repeating this bilge as the morons
they are. As long as there are conservative
respectables who will look stern and serious as
"progressives" recite their nonsense, the left is safe.
As long as conservative respectables say what True
Intellectuals and Honest Patriots leftists are, liberals
will survive and dominate our national dialogue. Conservative respectables live to oblige this leftist need.
What is important to a respectable conservative is to
maintain his respectability.

That is, after all, why respectable conservatives
are allowed national media exposure in the first place.

If a respectable conservative starts making a point
that bothers liberals, the "progressives" simply throw
frivolous   labels   at   him   like   "racist"   or
anaziwhowantstokillsixmillionjews. By the time he
has saved his respectability, he has completely forgotten the point he was making.

It never really mattered to him anyway.

It is not a conspiracy that selects kooks and light-
weights to be conservative media spokesmen. It is
simply that if you had someone there who would not
let liberals get away with silly stuff, the debate would
collapse and leftists would be humiliated.

A man who worked on a staff I headed for the

House Education and Labor Committee appeared once, just once, on a national television debate. The debate concerned increasing federal aid to education. My friend would not get off the point that the more federal aid there is the more student scores fall. The two liberals debating him were furious. They accused him of saying that giving money could actually HARM education — which was exactly what he WAS saying — and they were shouting that this was impossible.

They said education money HAD to help. My friend was pointing out that Federal money goes with federal regulation, and federal bureaucrats are ruining education.

There was a respectable conservative there who was a regular on the program. He was supposed to be on the same side as my friend. But this conservative respectable knew better than to join in this exposition of liberal silliness. The liberals were furious about it, and he had to satisfy them first.

He did so, and took their side against my buddy.

My buddy was, not surprisingly, never invited for another national debate anywhere. You will still see that conservative respectable on national television a lot.

The right will fail as long as it selects its spokesmen this way.

Respectable Conservatives Worship The "Neos"

Neoconservatives ("Neos") are the 1960's liberals who, around 1970, suddenly realized that public opinion was turning against leftism. So they switched sides.

In 1950, the word "liberal" was a compliment. By 1970, no one wanted to be called a liberal, even in New York politics. The real rats among the liberals could feel the water coming up around their necks. So they jumped ship by dropping the liberal label and started calling themselves "neoconservatives."

But neoconservatives insist they are still good leftists.

As one neoconservative put it, "I was a social democrat and I am a social democrat."

In the 1950s and 1960s people like me told the world that liberalism would lead to treason and policy disasters. Back then liberals, including the liberals who later became neoconservatives, said we were wrong. Those same neoconservatives still say that nothing liberals did before 1970 was wrong.

Neoconservatives say that one day about January 1, 1970, liberalism switched from absolute rightness to disaster. At that moment, the historical moment when liberalism went from Perfection to Evil, they became neoconservatives.

So neoconservatives say they were right to be liberals before and they were right to sell liberals out at exactly the correct historical moment.

Neoconservatives say that they were never just plain wrong. They say that before 1970 no one could have known that liberalism would go wild on or about January 1, 1970.

For many years before 1970 we told the world that liberalism was on the way to disaster. We said that liberalism was based on false premises that led to failure after failure.

Neoconservatives insist that they were right to stick with liberalism until on or about January 1, 1970. By that date liberalism became such an obvious failure and had brought on such obvious disasters that even neoconservatives saw it.

But neoconservatives insist they were right and folks like me were wrong right up to January 1, 1970.

Nothing is more natural than that respectable conservatives would worship neoconservatives. What could be more natural than for respectables who collaborate with liberals to worship the Neos who used to be big-time liberals?

Respectable conservatives were pathetically grateful when neoconservatives, who conservatives think of as big time people, began to associate with them. Before they switched sides neoconservatives got all the benefits of being liberals. In the 1960s many of them were high in the media and in the governmental and academic bureaucracies that conservatives were frozen out of. Respectable conservatives were thrilled that these neoconservatives who had once been bigwigs in the media and in government were now willing to have lunch with them. Respectable conservatives went nuts when neoconservatives started to WRITE for them.

Respectable conservatives could not believe that these Great Men who had previously only associated with liberal media moguls now talked to THEM!

As the hard-core liberal ship went down, conservatives not only welcomed the rats aboard the conservative ship, they gave them the helm.

As William Buckley keeps saying, "People talk about rats deserting the ship. Well, why shouldn't they?"

After all, some of those rats are his best friends.

David Horowitz screamed "racist" to prevent any opposition to his liberal stands on campus when he was a leftist. He is now the neoconservative who is in charge of the conservative side of the civil rights debate.

Horowitz never denies that, as a leftist, he helped crush all opposition to integration on campus by calling anyone who did not lie about race anaziwhowantedtokillsixmillionjews. Now he demands to know why there is not free speech on racial issues on college campuses.

According to neoconservatives, shrieking down all serious discussion of race before January 1, 1970, was the act of an Idealist, but on or about January 1, 1970, for no reason, it got ugly.

Forget Subtlety. The Problem Is Gross Dumbness

Respectable conservatives make their living by respectfully disagreeing with liberals.

We are in the same situation Dr. Semmelweis was in. We cannot deal with reality if we have any respect for this crap. Young Dr. Semmelweis had to tell the bigwigs in the Medical Profession that they had to forget their theories and wash their damned hands if they didn't want to kill patients.

Today we have to defrock and defund the professors and tell students who take them seriously, "Don't be an ass."

Liberalism is based on open fanaticism. Franz Boas didn't like the facts of anthropology so he founded a whole school called social anthropology. He openly dedicated that new "science" to proving the races were equal. He lied like a dog in his findings.

Margaret Mead and Dobzhansky and others in Boas' mutual admiration society invented what is now called "the American school of anthropology." It said "Whitey bad, non-whites good." They built their new "science" in American universities even though American university doctrine at that time was as conservative as its donors were.

But back then the conservative donors allowed universities to support Boas and his group because they could not bring themselves to suppress a different point of view.

Now social anthropology rules and they do not hesitate to crush any questioning of their position.

Most of the intellectual's big mistakes are unbelievably stupid.

The Bible came from Palestine so that is where most of the earliest archeology money went. Also, the Middle East was desert and little happened there, so digging was easy. So what happened next?

LO AND BEHOLD, MY BRETHREN! Archeologists discovered that everything had been invented right beside Palestine, to the west in Egypt or to the east in Mesopotamia. The rule became "Ex Oriente Lux," "From the East Comes Wisdom." It never occurred to these dumbasses that it was a hell of coincidence that they were finding everything right where they happened to be digging. After all, "Ex Oriente Lux" was the slogan of people who insisted they were intellectuals, so the last thing they could imagine was that they were making an obvious mistake.

We're still trying to climb out of that "Ex Oriente Lux" crap.

What color is sculpture? Well, all the sculpture they used to find was gray stone. So all the "sculptors" since did grey stone stuff and called it highly sophisticated art. There are "intellectuals" who advise Hollywood to make all the sculptures gray. The educational television series, "I, Claudius" had grey stone statues in his garden.

In "Mark Anthony," Richard Burton kept yelling, "Why do sculptures never have eyes?"

There wasn't any grey stone statuary in the Classical World. All the statues had eyes. They looked like statues at Madam Tussaud's, all painted to look as much as possible like real people. None of the real Roman or Greek statues even had brown eyes. They were blond and light and in living color. No professor mentions that in class. Few professors even know it.

The list goes on. If you see a movie showing soldiers marching through ancient Rome, Rome looks like one of the less well-to-do parts of Spanish Harlem. Every building is old and gray. The real ancient Rome

was wildly colorful, and by our standards mostly gar-
ish and in color combinations that would not appeal
to us.

A real anthropologist (not one of Franz Boas'
boys), Richard Leakey, was born and raised in Kenya.
He got tired of the rest of Africa getting all the credit
for early humans, so he dug in Kenya.

LO AND BEHOLD, MY BRETHREN!

Leakey found an early man in the form of an early
woman, right there where he chose to dig.

It turned out that mankind began right there in
Kenya, according to an endless stream of reports. I
wrote a letter to Science News about how stupid this
was and the flow of "this is where all mankind began" crap ended abruptly.

The list of simple boneheadedness on the part of
academia is endless. If someone will have a sense of
humor about how mindless academia is, we might
get some real history, some real anthropology, maybe
even some social programs that WORK

Part Five
The Politically Correct Hate List

Political Correctness Is Nothing New

We kept killing each other in the religious wars until we faced the fact that, no matter how many robes he's got on, a clergyman is just a man. Whenever you have intellectual tyranny, it is because somebody thinks he has a corner on the Truth.

You could not end Fascism or Communism until you realized that nobody had a monopoly on wisdom.

Any group that is allowed to tell itself that it has a special corner on Truth is going to start oppressing others.

We have an established religion in America. It is called Political Correctness. This is not news to most rational Americans.

What most Americans have not considered is where this religion comes from.

Political Correctness is publicly enforced and publicly financed through what is referred to as "higher education." From there it is spread by lower education, the media, and in every other area where college graduation is required.

To get a military commission or most other professional jobs in our society, one must go through what amounts to a liberal seminary. Universities in America have become liberal seminaries, schools for teaching the liberal or Politically Correct faith.

When I say liberalism is a religious faith I mean exactly that. As this book illustrates, nothing liberalism advocates has ever worked!

Those of us whose brains did not die in college are actually stunned by just how stupid academic ideas are.

In the 1950s those who said they were "intellectuals" almost universally agreed that socialism was
"the wave of the future." On campus it was almost
universally required doctrine that if the government
owned and ran all industry, the result would be not
only efficient but also fair.

Government ownership of the means of production and distribution was not only efficient. It was
also inevitable.

What this meant was that the "intellectual" would
take over the economy.

The result was that the third world was ruled by
"intellectual socialists" and two generations of people
lived in stagnant poverty while one Five Year Plan
after another failed. The human cost of that failure
was staggering.

So the destructive absurdity that was de rigueur
on university campuses in the 1950s was a direct
result of professors claiming that they were intellectuals and that they, the intellectuals, should rule the
world.

In the 1960s it was generally agreed among "intellectuals" that "so-called criminals" were actually
victims of society. All one needed to end crime was to
dump money into psychological programs, sociologi-
cal programs and education and the crime problem
would disappear.

In other words, the "intellectuals" should take
over the legal system.

The result of that policy was that felons were re-
peatedly let back out on the streets. The human cost
of this policy was staggering.

In the 1970s you were shunned on campus if
you believed that there were any genetic differences
in the behavior of men and women. If you took away
girls' dolls and boys' guns, the whole oppression of
females would end.

All that was needed was a huge infusion of money into sociology, psychology and education and women could go on to what John Galbraith called "the higher economic role of women."

Professors insisted that "It is as important for a woman to paint a picture as to have a baby." Many, many women followed that advice and lived to regret it bitterly.

Militant feminists do not like being reminded of their 1970s absurdities, so no respectable conservative ever mentions them.   The human cost of this nonsense was staggering.

The result has been the imposition of one policy after another that has been a total failure. Modern educational theories that got rid of phonics is another of many more examples.

Social science professors love to say they are the only True Voice of Humanity. But in the world I live in most of the real catastrophes were the direct result of fashionable opinion that came straight out of the universities.

But no matter how often they fail, liberal professors remain convinced they are the embodiment of true wisdom and true compassion. Their students believe that, and many never grow out of it.

And Now A News Bulletin About Mammoths

About ten thousand years ago there were mammoths in North America and giant sloths in South America. About that time the Indians crossed the land bridge into America.

It had always been taken for granted that "man destroyed the mammoths." I remember seeing pictures of white men in animal skins killing mammoths. It was the ice age, but everybody was depicted as being half naked, which was the symbol for "barbarian."

But when it came to North America, the historians have suddenly had a Revelation.

They had routinely condemned "Man" for killing the mammoths and showed those white guys doing it. Then it suddenly hit them that Man, in North America, meant Native Americans, those innocent lovers of Nature.

You could almost hear the "Screech!" of brakes as historians had to reassess this idea that Man destroyed the mammoths. The mammoths had existed through millions of years of ice ages and hot ages, but now the historians tell us that they died out naturally at exactly the time the Indians got here.

I am sure that we will soon be told that the Native Americans tried to save them.

Political Correctness Is A Game Of Trumps

The last chapter is not about mammoths. It is about the Blame Game of Political Correctness. We all know that Political Correctness blames everything Evil on Mankind.

But leftism also requires that all the sins of Mankind be the fault of the White Man. In contrast to the Evil White Man, non-whites are highly moral beings who are at one with Nature. This makes things a bit complicated, but modern history always adjusts instantly in order to make it fit into the Political Correctness scheme.

Fortunately, Political Correctness can count on the fact that no college graduate does any thinking at all. So when they showed white cave men killing mammoths while running around half naked in the Ice Age, nobody asked a single question.

So now when the image of Evil Mankind collides with the Noble Native American Who Loves Nature and who would not hurt Brother Mammoth, nobody asks about it.

When Indians came across the land bridge, mammoths, which had survived millions of years and a huge number of ice ages, just happened to drop dead.

So Politically Correct history is a lot like a game of trumps. Mankind is Evil, but that is trumped if the Mankind being referred to turns out to be non-white.

The Politically Correct Hate List

We have lived all our lives with this game of Politically Correct Trumps, but nobody has put down in detail exactly what the trumps are.

We all know that Political Correctness says that White Men are Evil and that Non-Whites are lovers of Nature and moral paragons.

Another rule of Political Correctness is "Animals good, People bad." So if man is greedy that is just awful. If an animal is greedy he is just following nature. When people destroy forests it is pure evil. When elephants destroy trees, it just shows how nice they are.

So we know these two rules: Whites Bad, non-Whites Good and People Bad, Animals Good.

But then we run into a case like the mammoths. When it was white men killing them, history declared man killed the mammoth. But if Man killed the mammoth in North America, then those men were non-white.

In this case "Man Bad, Animals Good" runs up against "White Man Bad, Indian Good."

Another rule of Political Correctness is "Poor People good, Rich People bad."

Political Correctness lives on Guilt, and there is no point in making poor people feel guilty because you can't get anything out of them. So the Virtuous Poor People are the victims of the Evil Rich.

You can get Guilt money out of the Evil Rich.

But what about a case where a person is a rich member of a minority? Here "White Man Bad, Minority Good" runs into "Rich People Bad."

Another rule of Political Correctness says, "Men

Evil, Women Good." We know that men who make unwelcome advances cause traumas that leave all women psychologically wrecked and ready for Oppression.

But what if the woman is white and the man is black?

White Bad, Black Good. So isn't it her fault for leading him on?

Rightist Mistakes Are Evil, Leftist Mistakes Are Just Too Idealistic

Leftists may be too idealistic, but they are never just plain hateful and stupid.

You have never heard any liberal admit that leftism was just plain wrong about anything.

You never will.

Political Correctness is never wrong, and therefore Political Correctness never admits that it had the wrong motives.

Only Rightists are hateful and stupid.

Every historian will tell you that all decent people always knew that women's rights were a good idea. It was just sexual impotence or meanness that made men oppress women.

Likewise black people.

Likewise animals.

So far it's easy.

But it gets dicey when we run into a case where historians have gotten everybody feeling guilty about the killing of the mammoths and then suddenly have to reverse course when they realize they are blaming the Nature Loving Native Americans for it.

Crimes against Political Correctness are always intentional.   For example, PC says that men oppressed women, not because they had the outlook of their own time and place, but because men felt impotent or were just plain bad.

PC explains that a slaveholder in 1750 was an evil man, not just a man who had been raised with slavery. At least ninety percent of the Confederate Army owned no slaves, but historians agree they fought and died just because they hated black people.

In other words, those who violate Political Correctness are Evil, not mistaken.

Like every other Inquisition, the Politically Correct Inquisition says that if you're wrong it is because you're Evil and you must be punished. But, like those who conducted every other Inquisition, the priests of Political Correctness can never be punished for being wrong.

After all, only Evil People are ever wrong. So no liberal is ever really wrong.

All Inquisitions Are Like This

Nazism depended heavily on selective breeding, race and genetics in general.

Communism depends just as entirely on the idea that genes mean nothing and a Communist world will make everybody equally smart and productive.

So when the Medicogenetic Institute of Moscow did the mother of all identical twin studies in the 1930s and found, as all such tests do, that heredity is vital, Stalin killed them.

To quote Soviet sources, the head of the Medicogenetical Institute, "confessed his ideological error and was shot."

In any Inquisition, ideological error can get you shot.

In the Middle Ages it was pretty routine for someone on the losing side of a theological argument to end up being burned alive if they did not recant. Even if half the Medieval theological experts believed one way and half believed the other way until the final decision, the half that was wrong was Evil and deserved punishment.

In 2001 a Polish court - a court in post-Communist Poland - determined that a particular concentration camp had been part of the Holocaust.

It is a felony in Poland to deny any aspect of the Holocaust. So the minute that the court decided that the concentration camp was part of the Holocaust, it became a felony to say it was not.

So the Polish lawyers who had argued against that concentration camp being in the Holocaust came into the building arguing one thing, but they could and WOULD have been arrested if they had said the same thing when they walked out after the decision.

Several French students who did research on the World War II period came to conclusions that ran afoul of the Holocaust law. They were threatened with imprisonment. The professors who oversaw their research were also threatened with prison.

These researchers and their professors actually cried on the witness stand. They confessed their ideological error, but they professed their complete orthodoxy. In other words, they acted like anyone facing Heresy charges under any Inquisition.

But this was not the Middle Ages and this was not the Soviet Union. This was Western Europe in the 1990s. Not one single liberal, American or European, saw the slightest problem with this. No academic, European or American, made the slightest objection.

For me, the idea of self-proclaimed academics in a so-called free country groveling and begging people not to put them in prison because they mistakenly contradicted the True Faith is really bone-chilling. Today's college student would wonder what bothers me about it.

All American media agree that Europe should be attacking the American death penalty, but no one here mentions that Europe's punishing Thought Crimes with prison might be bad.

A short time ago in Germany a scholar was on trial for saying that one concentration camp was not a death camp. The court declared that any technical witness for his side would face the mandatory one year in prison for Thought Crime.

I am the only person who even notices that all this is a Medieval throwback. That scares me more than the throwback itself.

Some readers will think I am beating this point to death. The average Yuppie or the average college student genuinely will not understand what I am upset about. I ask intelligent readers to bear with a paragraph more while I explain what I am talking about here to the Yuppies.

What I mean here is that, in a free country, if a lawyer defends someone and that person is convicted, no one requires the lawyer to admit the man is guilty. You would be terribly upset if every lawyer whose client got convicted was then required to admit his client was guilty or go to prison himself.   But in Europe once a court decides something is hate or some place is a death camp, a lawyer who says that isn't true goes to prison.

In The Crown Versus Joseph Pierce, 1986, the British court declared that, when it comes to contradicting racial orthodoxy, "The truth is no excuse." Try to imagine how outraged you Yuppies would be if they convicted a LEFTIST defendant for telling the truth!

What if a law said that anyone who said that Sacco and Vanzetti or O.J. Simpson were innocent would go to prison for it? Certainly a Yuppie could get upset about THAT.

This is the way I think of the European Hate Laws.

Most Yuppies still will not understand the connection. But it is necessary to keep trying to explain it. All the intellectual damage we call college education was not done in a day and it will not be repaired either quickly or easily.

In our Inquisition, Academic Freedom is one thing. Heresy is another. No American "intellectual" is going to object to European Hate Laws, no matter how many European professors end up weeping on the stand.

Academic freedom only protects leftist professors from the political right.

Questioning the left on campus is not academic

freedom. Questioning the left on campus is Heresy. You cannot allow Heresy in the name of academic freedom.

No one noticed this until recently, but it has been true since I entered college in 1957. So I am used to the fact that being Politically Incorrect ruins careers in America.

But in Europe Political Correctness "is not just a good idea, it is the law." That bothers me.

Political Correctness Is Not Like A State Religion, It IS Our State Religion

Nobody has any trouble with the idea that the Trial Lawyers' Association has some political prejudices. Nobody has any trouble believing that military personnel have political prejudices.

In fact, any reasonably intelligent person will see that almost any occupational group has its political preferences.

But the idea that social science professors are just humans who have professional political prejudices is never, never, never mentioned.

When professors talk about how greedy businessmen are, nobody ever asks the professors about their own greed.

And the last people on earth who could ever imagine that social science professors have professional biases are the social science professors themselves.

How can anyone be so blind? Very easily. People can be hopelessly stupid only if they are taught to believe that they are too smart to be judged by mere reality. I explain this in "When Dummies Try to be Shrewd" below.

People can be utterly merciless only if they have been trained to believe they are the only true humanitarians. The faith of Political Correctness, through the universities, teaches young people that their social science professors represent the Only True Intellectualism and the Only True Humanitarianism. Political Correctness is nothing new. It is our modern state religion. Every system of belief that is enforced by the state ends up being merciless.

Every system of belief that is enforced by the state

becomes merciless in the name of Mercy.

On campus, intolerance is routinely enforced in the name of Tolerance; diversity of opinion is routinely crushed in the name of Diversity.

State religion routinely suppresses real freedom in the name of True Freedom.

True Diversity and True Freedom are the battle cries of Political Correctness.

There is nothing new about those who preach our state-enforced religion. Professional academics sincerely believe that they simply cannot be fundamentally, catastrophically wrong.   Every religious priesthood, if left to itself, will become that way.

This is why it is impossible to understand Political Correctness if one thinks that modern academia is anything but the priesthood of America's state religion.

A religious faith is a belief in things without evidence. Liberalism and Political Correctness are things we are forced to believe against the evidence.

When I say liberalism is a religious faith, I mean it. I do not mean that Political Correctness is LIKE a religious faith; I mean it IS a religious faith.

By the same token, when I say that universities today are liberal seminaries I do not mean that universities today are LIKE liberal seminaries. I mean universities today ARE liberal seminaries.

Every religious seminary spends most of its time teaching general information, just like universities do. Universities teach history and other courses. Regular religious seminaries also teach Bible, languages, history and general theology. Like all religious seminaries, universities just put their own spin on all this information.

Like other religious seminaries, today's universities hire a few professors who are not of the faith they are teaching. Jewish professors teach at many major Christian seminaries, as do people of other faiths. Universities allow a very, very limited number of non-liberals to teach, but every single one of them has to swear his allegiance to the basic doctrines of Political Correctness.

Teachers are the natural choice to lead in the Inquisition, then and now. Two teaching orders, the Dominicans and the Jesuits, were charged with enforcing the Medieval Inquisition.

The difference between other religious seminaries and our liberal seminaries is that the public cannot be forced to finance any other religious school. But we all have to pay for liberal seminaries.

Our present Inquisition is simply a repeat of the old ones. Two Catholic orders were the "teaching orders" in the Catholic Church. They were the Dominicans and the famous Jesuits.

So guess what Orders were put in charge of enforcing the old Catholic Inquisition? The Dominicans and the Jesuits, of course.

But the Dominicans and the Jesuits had to fight to get control over schools by offering a good education. Even their enemies admitted they provided an excellent secular education and many Protestants sent their children to Jesuit schools for that reason.

Our Politically Correct priesthood provides a lousy education. Professors don't have to deliver anything and they don't. They have been given the dream of the Dominicans and the Jesuits on a silver platter. All education belongs to them from the get-go.

Colleges don't need required courses or anything else. All that counts is that they sign that accredited diploma, without which everybody's career is ruined.

You are not going to find the ACLU or any other group, liberal or conservative, taking this to court; but the simple fact is that we have an established religion and a set of seminaries on which we lavish

more public money and power than any other established religion on earth has ever enjoyed.

This is not just unconstitutional. This is outright
tyranny.

Our first step towards ending this tyranny is to
expose it. We have to start calling it tyranny, not An
Alternative Point of View.

We must have a revolution.

An Established Religion Always Destroys Precisely What It Claims To Champion

A Marxist Inquisition or a Catholic Inquisition both claim they know the Truth. When you know The Truth, it doesn't matter what is simply true. As Marx said, truth is a purely political matter.

When you refer to something as Truth, you are not talking about simple facts or simple truth. Let us put that more strongly: if you capitalize the word Truth, you are referring to something entirely different from simple reality, simple facts, and simple truth.

Exactly the same thing is true of the capitalized word Mercy. When the Medieval Inquisition tortured people to death, they did it in the name of Mercy. They could not show simple mercy because they were dedicated to the Higher Mercy of saving souls from eternal damnation.

In order to show true Mercy, an Inquisition must have no mercy. In order to spread Truth, one needs to suppress any inconvenient facts.

In 1903 Big Business set up monopolies. They opposed all restrictions on price fixing in the name of "Private Enterprise." The last thing a monopoly wants is private enterprise.

So a group that takes power in the name of Private Enterprise will be an enemy of real, uncapitalized private enterprise. A Church that says it represents Truth is the worst enemy the simple truth can have.

A Church that says it represents Mercy will be merciless.

An established religion that calls itself Education is the worst enemy education can have. You can take it for granted that a power group that hides be-

hind the term Academic Freedom suppresses any
serious diversity of opinion.

Nonviolent Thugs

In an indecent society the thugs are violent. In a decent society most of the thugs use our decency against us.

Which kind of thug is worse, the one who is violent in an indecent society or the one who uses a people's very decency against them?

Violent thugs are open bullies. Nonviolent thugs call themselves wonderful and loving pacifists.

Both kinds of thugs are true lowlifes.

When I was in high school there was a little guy who made life miserable for all of us on the football team. One day I pointed out to him that he was a bully.

"I'm too little to be bully," he said. I explained to him that a bully is a person who uses his size to make life hard for other people. He did things to us that we would fight about with anybody else, but he could do them because he was so small we would be ashamed to fight him.

Here is the unbelievable part: This guy listened and changed his behavior. If he had been a college student or a college graduate who never outgrew his college education he would have insisted that he was no bully. He would say he was just exercising his rights as a Size-Challenged Person.

He had not been to college yet. In college he would have learned that professors represent the only True Free Speech, the Only True Mercy, and the Only True Compassion. Professor Knows Best.

Fortunately this follow was not in college. He realized from what I said that a little guy is not helpless in a decent society. He was decent enough to take that to heart.

Our Politically Correct Inquisition uses every de-
vice it can find to cripple that kind of morality. This
little guy was just one more South Carolina Bible
Belter who didn't want to hurt anybody. The priests
of Political Correctness would have tried to make him
a weapon for their purposes.

So in our school, this guy fit in because he was a
decent person. We had big people and we had little
people. That was probably a kind of diversity, but we
didn't really think of it that way.

That kind of diversity is a million miles from
today's Diversity.

Instead of welcoming blind people into society,
Political Correctness uses blind people to cripple free
speech. Our professor-priests tell us that, for the sake
of blind people, we must never use words like "I see"
for "I understand."

If you control language you control dissent.

In a decent society the thugs can use that decency to destroy the mainstream. Every disabled person becomes a tool of the Language Police. Every small
person becomes a tool of the Language Police. Above
all, every member of a minority becomes a member
of the Language Police.

This is not mainstreaming. This is a capitalized
disease called Mainstreaming, which makes everybody a special case to be defined by the "intellectuals."

What Would We Do If Any Other Religion Took Over Our Schools?

How dare I say all this?

Many will insist on my proving that professors are biased before I talk about the implications of social science bias. A good respectable conservative would demand to know how I DARE talk about an Established Religion without even writing a book to show that social science professors have prejudices in the first place.

A good respectable conservative would begin by trying to prove this fact. There have been many respectable conservative books devoted to proving some groups have a liberal bias. So no respectable conservative starts with what people already know and talks about the implications of what everybody already knows.

As I have explained, I am not a respectable conservative. So I will simply press the point that, if you base your world view on the idea that there are as many conservative professors as liberal ones, you're nuts.

I respect people who sincerely believe the world was created in six days, but I cannot discuss this proposition with them. I don't try. Likewise, there are people who genuinely believe professors have no biases. I cannot discuss this proposition with them. I don't try.

If you believe the earth was created in six days, you have a religious faith. If I say the world was created in six days, I am having delusions and need care.

If you believe professors today are objective observers whose only interest is in the truth, you may believe it. I have paid taxes all my life to pay for the faculties who taught you that. If you believe it, it's not your fault.

But if I even act like I take that idea seriously, I need psychiatric care.

This book explains what conservatives never go into, that is, "What are the implications of the fact that professors are so biased that they constitute a political priesthood?"

The first step in dealing with our established national religion is seeing it clearly as an established religion. So what do we do now?

What would we do if any OTHER religion took over our schools?

If a Catholic Inquisition took control over our tax money and our young people through the state, would we denounce all opposition to it as anti-Catholic? But any questioning of our present established religion is called anti-intellectual.

Cleaning out the universities is our right, since we pay for them and~~~~~our children attend them. They are OUR schools.

Using public institutions to advance a political agenda that amounts to an established religion is not something that can be opposed moderately or respectfully.

And the last thing such a revolution would be is anti-intellectual. There is nothing intellectual about today's social science and the religion of Political Correctness. Today's established religion on campus is the enemy of any kind of real thought or any true intellectualism. On social science faculties today the intellectual has been totally displaced by the True Believer.

Social science today is SILLY. It is inbred. It is a religious orthodoxy. There is no place for it in our society. We must clean our academic stables if we ever want Johnny to be able to think again.

Part Six
How Leftists Will Fight Academic Reform

Academia Is Ready To Fail Its Second Test

My argument in this book is that social scientists are too inbred and too professionally biased to be given the money and power they have without any outside interference.

One reaction to this observation is for the person I am talking to to run interference, to block it. He blocks anyone from addressing my point by accusing me of fascism, racism, Hate, wanting to suppress true freedom of thought, child molesting and halitosis.

To run interference against this simple observation, you have to concentrate on every word I say here and how I say it. You have to argue over each instance I cite. The general argument I make and the obvious conclusions I come to about academia must be obscured in any way possible.

If the people who call themselves "intellectuals" were really social scientists, I wouldn't have to write this book in the first place. There is nothing here that a real social scientist wouldn't have taken for granted at least fifty years ago. It is a social scientist's job to study occupational prejudices. He should have started by studying his own.

So social science has failed the first test. This is a group of people whose lunch I pay for so they will have nothing to do but figure out human biases, and it never occurred to them that they themselves have any.

That's about as obvious a test as any profession can fail.

Instead of thinking about things that matter, academics spend their time, the time I pay for, impressing each other.

Even college graduates are beginning to realize that there is something rotten in academia. Good liberals never will see that.

Liberals are and always will be intellectual six-year-olds. They will never understand that there is anything really wrong with academia.

Conservatives often reach a mental age of ten. They know something is wrong with professors, but they insist that professors are professionals and must be respected. Professors can't be doing anything that is just plain silly.

Conservatives assume that professors are dedicated and slightly misguided. They say that all professors need to do is to be even nicer than they already are.

So everybody is on board. Professors are wonderful, idealistic, well-meaning people who just need to control themselves. They should be the fair, compassionate, loving and truly intellectual professionals that college graduates are taught to think they are.

Meanwhile, back on Earth, the truth is very simple: professors have not been kept in line so they've gone ape. The same thing happened to Big Business when Teddy Roosevelt started his Trust Busting. The same thing happened to medicine when public revulsion made them stop killing people by bleeding them.

Now that their heroes have been caught abusing their power, liberals are going to do what every political group does when its favorite peoples' errors are exposed.

Instead of facing the fact that social scientists have been caught acting human, liberals are going to stonewall.

In the end, nothing but a revolution will actually

do what needs to be done.

After Stonewalling, Social Scientists Will Fall Back On "Self-Regulation"

So the failures of leftism largely derive from the fact that social scientists are human beings. The people we pay to analyze human prejudices never discuss their own.

The people we pay to know about human reactions are having their own biases exposed. Now those who call themselves "scientists" in just this area are going to what every group does when its biases are revealed. Leftists are going to stonewall and dicker over every word I say and every instance I cite. They are going to fight to avoid discussing the obvious reality I am referring to.

This is the technique called "spin" or "running interference." It means using any tactic to avoid the simple question: "Do social scientists want professors to rule the world?" or "Does the profession that calls itself social science have any general biases at all?"

"Spin" is an obvious technique. It is a childish technique. It is a method of lying.

The interference technique is so obvious that decent people are ashamed to use it. So most people who have to listen to what I say just admit that social science has its biases like any other occupation. Once I point this out and refuse to back down, the usual reply is that of course it's true.

When they run out of stonewalling techniques, liberals will admit that professors, like every other occupational group, have biases.

Now we get to Phase Three: What is to be done about social science biases?

Once again, the people who get paid to know all

about human history and human motivations are going to do exactly what every group in history has done when someone exposes their biases and they can't stonewall any more.

They will say, "So we made some mistakes. Leave it to us. We'll fix it."

They are going to say, "We are the experts on social science. We will reform ourselves."

They will say, "You are not experts in social science. Who the hell are you to say how we should reform the social sciences?"

They will say, "Anybody who tries to reform us from the outside is Anti-Intellectual and an Enemy of Academic Freedom."

Which is exactly what every other monopoly in history said at this stage.

Sure professors need to reform. But they can do it themselves.

Just leave it to the professors to reform, say leftists. Let them regulate themselves.

I have spent a lot of years dealing with regulation.

When I was in international aviation negotiations (I love to say that! It sounds like I owned Delta!) the Civil Aeronautics Board (CAB) was supposed to regulate airline fares.

The CAB was supposed to keep air fares reasonable and the airlines in check, all in the public interest.

Meanwhile, back on Planet Earth, the CAB was the property of the airlines and everybody knew it.

Likewise it was well known that the Interstate Commerce Commission was the creature of the industry they were supposed to control. If the Interstate Commerce Commission ever did anything that the big transportation companies didn't want done, it was before living memory.

Regulators routinely end up belonging to the industry they are supposed to regulate. It is hard enough to regulate an industry when you have an official government regulator. Before you get a regulator, the pretense is even shallower.

Social scientists don't have a regulator yet. They haven't even reached Phase 1 and noticed their own giant, ridiculous biases yet. This book is an early part of Phase 1. They will ignore the whole thing for quite a while to come.

Phase 2 is stonewalling.

So it will be quite a while before they get to Phase 3, the "We will regulate ourselves" bit.

And remember, what social scientists insist that the government should not regulate is what the government is paying for.

In the end, nothing less than a revolution will do the job.

What Is This So-Called "Self-Regulation?"

One of the sweetest deals around that calls itself "self-regulation" is the Better Business Bureau. They investigate nothing. If customers complain they will keep complaints on file and you can read them if you have lots of time to spare.

Have you ever seen a Better Business Bureau warn the public about any business?

Professors of hard science have an effective form of outside regulation. If they start talking nonsense, buildings fall down and planes crash.

But social science always fails and nobody wants to "interfere" with them.

Professors say that, in the name of Academic Freedom, they will regulate themselves.

What businesses call self-regulation is what social science professors call "peer review." "Peer review" means that only social scientists will decide what gets published in the social sciences. "Peer review" means that the only people who decide who will be in the next generation of social science professors is this generation of social science professors.

If any other group of people besides professors said they should live on your money without any interference from you, you would be suspicious. In this case, no student is ever suspicious. In this case nobody who got a college education and never grew out of it is going to be suspicious of academic "self-regulation."

So what exactly is this so-called "self-regulation?"

This "self-regulation" or Free Enterprise or Academic Freedom dodge is the standard next stage of the standard process. First, a cartel gets caught abusing power in crazy ways like academia does to-day or monopolistic businessmen did in 1900.

At the end of the first stage, even the business-men or professors have to admit that their cartel be-havior has gone nuts and is destroying the very things it is supposed to nurture.

In the "self-regulation" stage, the big business cartel or the professors' associations come up with a very complicated plan that ends up leaving things exactly the way they were when the so-called reform started.

The Big Railroads were caught fixing railroad prices, so they set up the Interstate Commerce Com-mission to set prices for them. Businesses caught conspiring and doing other things set up the Better Business Bureaus, another toothless watchdog that keeps away public scrutiny of small business.

So when academic "self-regulation" starts, the pretense will be huge. There will be impressive Con-sulting Committees and similar crap coming to the universities. Professors can't figure out their own bi-ases, but they sure as hell will find a way to keep their power and their money.

So let's get back to basics. Medicine killed people by the millions by bleeding them to death and caus-ing infections by cutting them for bleeding. This did not stop because of a compromise.

There was no compromise between bleeding and bacteriology. For decades people died because offi-cial spokesmen ran interference for University Doc-tors who championed the Humor Theory of Galen.

My father owned a brick plant. If he was at a convention and mentioned the price of brick, he could have gone to prison for it under federal anti-trust laws. My father was very conservative politically and he didn't like that rule, but he was one hundred per-cent in favor of it.

As the prophet of real private enterprise, Adam Smith, said in 1776, businessmen cannot talk about prices without fixing them.

When I was on Capitol Hill, I listened to a patriot who had won the Congressional Medal of Honor testify on military policy.   He was a fine man, but I didn't just automatically believe what he told me. No one can be trusted on military policy if he is a professional. If you let him set policy, you will throw away tax money. If you trust him to decide on the use of the military on his own, you are risking a military dictatorship.

When it comes to public money or public power, self-regulation is NEVER a good idea.

Does that include Academic Freedom for people who get paid to sign college degrees?

What part of the word "NEVER" are you having trouble with?

The most wonderful people in everything else become mean and nasty beyond imagination if they are allowed to pursue their professional interests without intrusive regulation.

I said "intrusive" regulation.

Repeat: "Intrusive."

Liberals cannot regulate professors because they think professors are wonderful and practically perfect.

Conservatives cannot regulate professors because they think professors are wonderful but somewhat flawed. The media will not accept anyone as a Respectable Conservative Spokesman unless he shows respect for professors.

Once again, medicine could not begin saving lives until the last person running interference for bleeding therapy was laughed out of the profession. The only way to prevent the most honest businessman from fixing prices is Draconian punishment and banning all discussion of prices at business meetings

No one can intrusively regulate professors except people who cause professors to scream bloody murder.

In the end nothing less than revolution will do the job.

The Left Needs Regulation Just Like The Right Does

The media says that Private Enterprise is an over-used term. The media points out that every time a business abuses its power, "private enterprise" or "the free market" is thrown up as an excuse.

But the media says that terms like Academic Freedom cannot be overused. The left has also made "freedom of the press" into a leftist cliché.

Since the media moved left after World War II, "freedom of the press" has become a byword on that side of the spectrum. It is often implied that the press should be free not only from regulation but from criticism. The media should only regulate itself.

When other big businesses got to the size of our media today, the old Adam Smith "free enterprise" argument was no longer sufficient. When a handful of big businessmen could control all steel production in a private conversation, self-regulation was no longer sensible.

But almost every city in America has a monopoly newspaper, and everybody insists this is the exactly the same "freedom of the press" as it was back when anybody could set up a little printing press and every sizable city had several dailies.

In earlier days big business monopolies hid behind "Private Enterprise" exactly the same way that newspaper monopolies hide behind "Freedom of the Press" today.

Liberals agree that Big Media, including the movie industry, is the only gigantic private enterprise that should be entirely "self-regulating." Any outside regulation of a media giant is Censorship.

And, of course, liberals insist that any self-styled

"artist" who calls himself a "revolutionary" or "dissi-
dent," meaning leftist, should get government money.
Attacking the media monopoly is an attack on Freedom of the Press. Denying public money to a self-
proclaimed leftist Artist is Censorship.

You can explain the difference between censorship and refusing someone a public grant until you
are blue in the face, but a leftist simply, honestly has
no idea what you are talking about.

In the end nothing less than a revolution will do
the job.

If You Want To Take Money From Children, You Call Yourself An "Artist"

There is no big mystery as to the reason that professors are leftists. Leftism means professors rule the world. A social science professor is the only person who can spend most of his time saying that he should rule the world and get paid for it.

So why are artists and actors so often leftists?

Do artists have any natural ideological preferences?

Whenever a discussion begins on the Federal financing of "art," the media people discussing the subject get that Look of Constipated Seriousness on their faces and say, "How do you define Art?"

Actually, the definition of Art for Federal funding is very simple:

In order to get Federal funding "Art" has to be something somebody wants to do but nobody wants to pay for. So in order to get federal financing, "art" cannot depend on anybody wanting to look at it. If anybody wants to look at it you don't have to get a federal grant.

According to liberal theory, every government nickel that goes into "art" comes out of the pockets of seriously needy people. Government financing has to balance the money it gives to feeding children with the money it has to give to finance a Modern Work of Art like *The Intimate Commode* or *Piss Christ*.

Money for "art" comes out of the money that would go to social programs. So artists demand a lot more money for social programs.

The simple fact is that if you produce art that people want to have or look at, you don't need to define the word "art." If you produce art for art's sake, you don't need to define it as "art."

People start demanding to be called "artists" when they want to get paid for something others don't want to pay for. The Internal Revenue Service will go and force people to pay for your stuff if the government declares that what you do is Art. You get a teaching job at taxpayer expense if you get declared to be an expert in Art.

But somebody who demands to be called an Artist does not produce art for art's sake. If your art is its own reward, why do you need a title?

The market system, what "Artists" call Commercialism, has done good things for audiences. They get what they want to see at prices they are willing to pay.

America's entertainment industry may be criticized in many ways, but is popular everywhere.

Commercial entertainment is good for the audience but it is very hard on actors. Most actors live on starvation wages and a few make millions. But the few who make millions are under a lot of pressure and may fail tomorrow.

In the actors' and artists' dream society, they would get paid to do what they want to do. They would have job security.

Everybody would rather do what they want to do and get paid for it instead of doing what they have to do to earn money.

But actors want to be paid to be Artists. If every actor were officially declared to be an Artist, he would keep his income and fame and do whatever he wanted to do. That's the way it was in the Soviet Union. Roosevelt's New Deal included a massive Arts program.

What people believe is mostly a product of what they want to believe. So an actor will never say, "I want to do whatever I want to do and get paid for it."

Instead, he says he is against Commercialism.

In plain English, what actors call Commercialism is doing what people are willing to pay them to do. It is to be expected that most actors secretly ache for a system like that in the Soviet Union where every actor and dancer is a civil servant. You can only do that in a Communist system where Commercial Entertainment is outlawed.

In the real world, Soviet state-sponsored entertainment cannot compete with the real thing. The minute Soviet "entertainment" came up against Western, Evil, Commercial entertainment, it collapsed.

Damned few people in Russia today pay to see the movies seventy years of Soviet "artists" produced.

Actors don't want to believe in Commercialism because Commercialism makes life hard for them. The free market makes things hard for everybody. We would all rather get paid for doing what we want to do instead of what people want to pay us to do.

Naturally actors are leftists. There is nothing evil about this.   They want to get paid and do what they want to do. That is a normal, natural, and very human point of view.

The problem is that if actors get paid for what they want to do it means people have to be forced to pay for shows they don't want to pay for and watch shows they don't want to watch.   Those who denounce Commercialism in Art say that the peasants need that kind of discipline. The left says that the people need Art Experts to tell them what to do.

That kind of thinking produces countries people want to escape from.

In the year 1903, big businessmen had the same attitude that today's actors do. They wanted to produce whatever they wanted to and force people to pay for it. So the big businessmen liked to fix prices and stop having to compete with each other.

Today we like to think that the big business price
fixers of 1903 were especially evil or especially greedy.
They weren't especially evil or especially greedy, they
were just human beings.

If we had let big business keep fixing prices back
then, America today would be a country people would
want to escape from instead of a country people want
to immigrate to.

It doesn't matter whether you call it Socialism or
Free Enterprise, if you let people force other people
to pay them to do what they want to do things get
very, very bad for everybody.

The Media Says "We're Just Too Good To Be True"

Nobody wants regulation to interfere with his monopoly.

This is true of corporations. Back in 1903, when Big Steel magnates sat around a table fixing prices, they said that they had the right to be free of government price regulation because of the sacred rights of private property.

But none of those Big Steel magnates were interested in the sacred rights of private property if it would interfere with their monopoly.

If workers tried to organize against Big Steel, Big Steel demanded the government send in troops. If people wanted to import cheaper steel, nobody was more in favor of government tariffs than American Big Steel.

Today the National Education Association (NEA) says it believes firmly in Academic Freedom.

Until it comes to home schooling. At that point, the NEA demands the government outlaw its competition.

Big Media demand total freedom of speech.

Until it comes to the right of somebody else to get a station license.

Two things every industry wants:

1) Its own freedom to self-regulate; and

2) The government to protect it from competition.

On point 1), all the occupations are pretty straightforward. Everybody demands "self-regulation," which means fake reforms or no changes at all, in the name of "freedom."

Rightists demand that business be free of government in the name of free enterprise. When professors get paid to push their idea that professors should rule the rule, they call it "academic freedom."

The media protects its monopolies in the name of Freedom of the Press.

Today's college graduate sincerely believes that corporations use clichés like private enterprise to cover abuses, scandals, and power-grabs. But the same college graduate is incapable of imagining that when the left says "academic freedom" or "censorship" or Freedom of the Press, you should watch out for abuses, scandals, and power-grabs.

So when any profession is abusing its power, it wants government to butt out. It uses code terms like private enterprise, freedom of the press, fighting censorship, and so forth, but it all means "I'm getting mine, so you stay out of my way."

When any powerful profession is faced with losing its privileges, it tells the government to butt in. There comes a time when every power group says to the government, "Protect my privileges."

Once again, they don't say "Protect my privileges" in plain English. There is a code for "Protect my privileges" that is as old as the hills.

The code for "protect my privileges" is

1) "I am a professional"; and

2) "The government needs to protect the public from non-professionals."

In 1903, Big Steel did not say, "Protect our monopoly." Big Steel said, "Tariffs are patriotic" and "We must protect Americans from shoddy imports."

As education fails, people seek alternatives. Home schooling is a growing threat to the public education monopoly. But the NEA does not say, "We want the government to protect our monopoly." The National Education Association says "The government must protect children from non-professionals in education."

But there is one big difference between the "professional" excuse when conservatives use it and the same excuse when liberals use it. If liberals use the old "professional" excuse, they are BELIEVED.

Twenty years ago the left had a lock on the national media. CBS, NBC and CBS were solidly left, and PBS was even farther left. Now the Federal Communications Commission cannot protect the networks from growing competition.

The old inbred leftist journalism bureaucracy will never admit it is just inbred and noncompetitive. So what do they say they are?

They're "professionals."

So what do the media say the real problem is?

Lack of professionalism, of course.

The liberal Washington Post had a writer who got a Pulitzer Prize and had to give it back because her story was a complete fraud.

Everybody agreed that that scandal was not the fault of the Washington Post.

That scandal only occurred because non-professionals were ruining the media.

This is the line that was repeated by every liberal and agreed to by every respectable conservative: The Washington Post had been forced to accept those fake stories because of competition from tabloids and other non-professionals.

The Idealists at the Washington Post "were just trying too hard to compete."

Poor babies!

Recently the New York Times found that a reporter had been handing in totally false reports for years.

All the news panels agreed that this was just a temporary lapse. The Times had to compete with the sensational tabloids.

If a tabloid had wild scandals like that, people

would suspect a pattern of abuse existed. But every-body agrees the Times and the Post are professionals and this is a one-time thing.

If any institution has everybody covering for them that way, how often are they going to get caught? The reporters who caught the New York Times let those false reports go on for years and reported their suspicions only inside the Times.

Liberal reporters pointed out that there had been INTERNAL reports about the lying going on at the New York Times for months. That was supposed to prove how honest peole at the New York Times are.

So did the respectable conservatives point out that showed how DISHONEST they were? Did con-servatives point out that that just showed how lying is protected inside the liberal newspapers?

Of course not! They said the New York Times and Washington Post are paragons of honest report-ing.

So who is going to report it when the liberal me-dia puts out false information?

Every liberal and every respectable conservative spokesman agrees that the New York Times would never let any more false stories in, because they are professionals. Every Yuppie believes that. No college student questions that.

So professional media people are not just unbi-ased, they are superhuman. They are fighting to pro-tect us from the non-professionals.

So why would anyone say bad things about these wonderful professional news people?

Obviously, the only reason you would criticize the professional media people is because you are being unfair.

The media tell us they are criticized because they fearlessly report bad news.

The only reason anybody ever objects to "professional," meaning liberal, journalists is because they bring bad news. Ah, they sigh, it is a hard thing to be the bearer of evil tidings, but that is the burden we practically perfect people must bear.

No conservative has ever been known to say a word about how silly this excuse is. Respectable conservatives sit there with that look of constipated seriousness they always have on their faces when liberals say something laughable.

The media say people don't like them because they have to report the bad news. Meanwhile, back on Planet Earth, they give out precious little bad news about themselves or their favorites.

Actually the "professional journalists" report little if any bad news about the media themselves or about professors or about the misuse of money by big foundations. There is damned little bad news about any liberal profession.

And if any leftist lapses have to be admitted, they are explained away very quickly. And they are the exception.

But no conservative will ever mention any of this if he wants to be a Respectable Conservative Spokesman.

Actually the liberal media and the big foundations are perfect examples of occupational groups that

1) insist on self-regulation; and

2) make the government enforce their cartel privileges.

Leftists have become past-masters of taking over big money foundations. They are full-time professionals at it. They get paid for it. There is hardly a single big-money tax-deductible group that does not belong to a group of leftists.

Leftists control all that money and insist on their right to self-regulate how they use it.

But the key word here is "tax-deductible." These

are foundations because they are centrally controlled under rules set down by the government. Once you get them, you have them forever.

The government enforces that. We taxpayers pay a major portion of the cost of that.

The government recognizes accreditation as the sole right of the education cartel. To be an army officer you have to have an accredited degree. To work for a government contractor you have to have accredited credentials. Only professors are allowed to choose professors, and the government enforces that.

I pointed out earlier that the Egyptian Pharaoh used to perform a ceremony every morning to be sure the sun rose. I added that, on the plus side, the Egyptian sun did indeed come up every single day.

Professors get paid so that they will give students accredited diplomas. Johnny can't think, but Johnny has that diploma, which means he is officially "educated."

Nobody noticed when colleges stopped having required courses, because the diplomas came out no matter what and the professors got paid no matter what.

So the professor-priesthood makes sure people get an official education, just as the Pharaoh made sure the sun came up.

The sun came up. Johnny gets his degree.

Johnny can't think because he has to be "educated."

It's not just a good idea. It's the law.

Hardy's Law

We all still know about the great 1920s comedy team Laurel and Hardy. Oliver Hardy was the fat one, the boss of the moronic duo.

The real Oliver Hardy was born and raised in Augusta, Georgia. He got his background on how people act while being reared in his mother's boarding house, with all the guests and characters there. Hardy was a wise old Southerner at an early age.

It took real art to make the Oliver Hardy character one you could laugh at and actually like. After all, it would have been very easy to play him as just a big, mindless bully pushing little Stan Laurel around.

Hardy made his character funny instead of boorish. He told a reporter the big secret of why Oliver Hardy was so laughable. You see, little Laurel always freely admitted he was dumb and always asked Hardy to be his leader. But Hardy actually thought he was smart enough to know what they should do. So the real Oliver Hardy stated the wisdom that made his character so hilarious. He said,

"NOBODY IS AS FUNNY AS A DUMB MAN WHO THINKS HE'S SMART." And that is exactly what I mean when I capitalize the word "SHREWD."

Liberal Hicks

In 1977 I was at a party on Capitol Hill. I had just published a book that made some waves so I was a temporary sensation. A member of Senator Kennedy's staff was at the party and he wanted to ask me a question.

"Bob," he said, "You're a Southerner and you know your stuff. Tell me, is Jimmy Carter SMART?"

The reason he wanted to know about James Earl Carter, of course, was because said Jimmy Carter had just been inaugurated as President of the United States. Carter had come from nowhere and he had rolled over all the big Democratic names to do so. Those big names included one Senator Teddy Kennedy of Massachusetts.

This guy regarded his boss, Senator Ted Kennedy, as mental giant. He was asking me what every Northern Democrat was asking about Carter: Could a Southern white man be SMART?

It was a party, so I didn't give my usual acid reply to the question a dithering idiot asks me. I just said, "Man, he's PRESIDENT."

I am sure the Kennedy man thought it was a very naive answer and decided that was what he got for asking a white Southerner for advice.

Four years later, liberals had just been run over by Ronald Reagan in the 1980 election. They had been destroyed like a rabbit hit by a freight train. So they were assuring each other that Reagan was actually dumb.

For eight years Reagan kept running over the liberals and they kept assuring each other that Reagan was dumb and they were Shrewd. The media took up the cry, "Reagan DUMB!"

When Ronald Reagan took office in 1981, Michael Gorbachev was head of the only other Superpower on earth. By the time Reagan got through with him, Gorbachev had not only lost the Cold War, but his country no longer existed.

So every time liberals try to prove Reagan had nothing to do with the fall of the Soviet Union, guess who they quote?

They quote Michael Gorbachev, who assures them that Reagan wasn't all that bright.

Laurel and Hardy, Professors And The Media

Professors don't say they're SHREWD. They say they're "sophisticated." Neither professors nor the media have ever gotten over the fact that after Harvard Think Tanks got us into Vietnam, it was under Ronald Reagan that Communism collapsed.

Professors could never get used to the idea that Reagan could handle foreign policy. That's because he didn't seem "sophisticated," a.k.a., SHREWD.

Anything that confuses the professors totally blitzes the media. The only education media spokesmen have, after all, is the one that made them half-baked products of the professors. That's the only thing newsmen ever had that could be called an "education."

That's why newsmen are almost all liberals.

The Hardy character thought he was smart, so he convinced poor little Laurel that he was smart. Like the media and the professors, Hardy was the only example of "smart" poor dumb Laurel had, and the professors were the only "education" media spokesmen ever had.

So exactly like Laurel believed in Hardy, the media BELIEVE in professors.

In his book, Bias: A CBS Insider Exposes How the Media Distort the News, Bernard Goldberg makes a critical point with the clarity that only a person who has been inside the process can attain.

Goldberg explains that the editors of the big media don't get together each morning with some plot to advance the liberal agenda. Reporters and the media are not really aware that there IS a liberal agenda. All they have ever heard is that you must feed hungry children, open the borders up for third world immigration, provide medial care for old people, impose racial quotas, penalize business monopolies and do other good things.

As Goldberg says, reporters don't think they're leftist, they just think they're "realistic." Journalists never mature beyond the day they got their diploma at the end of their college indoctrination. Why?

Because journalists have exactly the same problem that professors do. Professors can never imagine that they are just being silly because they see themselves as the ultimate in mental power and knowledge. Likewise, reporters think they don't just KNOW reality, they ARE reality, because they report on the world.

Contrary to what you might think, it is easy to remain naive if you are on the scene of the action. More than one photographer has stood there and recorded his own shooting. He just couldn't feel that what he was photographing affected him, even after the bullet hit him. Reporters are every bit as inbred as professors. They are judged only by other reporters and former reporters. They ride together, they talk together. They promote each other.

Just as professors believe in their own words as the final truth to a hypnotic extent, so do reporters.

Neither journalists nor professors can ever grow up. Neither journalists nor professors can see themselves and their colleagues as anything less than Reality itself.

Nothing less than a revolution can unseat them.

Peter Seller's last movie was a replay of the old fairy tale, "The Emperor's New Clothes." It describes today's situation perfectly.

What is hilarious is how Peter Seller's last movie, "Being There," so perfectly described today's reporters and professors. If someone else put out the excuses and nonsense the media take for granted, it would immediately be identified as moronic drivel.

Peter Seller's character in "Being There" was severely mentally retarded. His name was Chauncey and he happened to be taken in by a wealthy and influential family in Washington. Chauncey said he was a gardener so everybody called him Chauncey Gardener.

What Gardener said sounded like the driveling of a moron, but everybody knew he couldn't be a retard because this powerful and wealthy family had taken him in. Gardener was There, right There at the top of the ladder. So what seemed to be idiotic drivel had to be Obscure Truth.

So everybody assumed that Chauncey was being profound. As the saying goes, "It sounds profound, but it is actually meaningless."

Just because a reporter is a moron doesn't mean he is lying. If he says, "Noise loud," you can assume it was indeed a loud noise. But the minute anything requires thought, he falls into the groove retarded people have to use. Reporters say China is poor because of White Exploiters. That was what the professors said when they were in college and reporters will go on repeating that the rest of their lives.

A reporter could watch someone shot down trying to escape across the Berlin Wall and write only about Hitler as an Evil German. His professor said Hitler was bad and Communists are idealists, and he will go on saying that for the rest of his life.

Reporters were right there at the 1968 Tet Offensive in Viet Nam. They described it as very loud, which it was. They said "Noise loud," and they spoke the truth.

But the media also almost unanimously reported that the Tet Offensive was a victory for the Viet Cong, which was dead wrong. But that was what their colleagues told them at the Saigon bar where reporters got together.

In 1968, the press was solidly against the Vietnam War. But in 1968, when Israel attacked the USS Liberty, not one single Brave Reporter said one single word about it.

But none of this is because you have to be a lazy, mindless coward to get by in the news business. They're all heroes, you know.

They just CAN'T be a bunch of Chauncey Gardeners!

Can they?

The Olympic Champions Of "Shrewd"

I worked in a prison. Unlike most prisons, this was not a fun place.

But there was one thing everybody enjoyed, and that was The New Psychologist. This was the '60s, and nobody was a True Believer like The New Psychologist. He had just finished a college degree and a master's and an internship surrounded by Intellectuals who trained him in the idea that every inmate was a Victim.

He was told that Society lied, but Victims of Society told the truth.

And the New Psychologist Believed, my God, did that man Believe!

Inmates would come out of sessions with the New Psychologist purple with suppressed laughter. They couldn't wait to tell everybody what they had told The New Psychologist and what he said back.

They simply couldn't say anything so stupid that the New Psychologist didn't believe them!

That boy gave us all joy.

You see, the New Psychologist Truly Understood the inmates. He was too Shrewd to think like the rest of us did. He was educated.

I hate to get provincial on you, but I don't believe you have seen a real New Psychologist until you have seen a SOUTHERN New Psychologist. Northern Yuppies are funny, but the World Champion of Shrewd is a Southern Liberal.

Since the 1960s even the New Psychologist has gotten a little cynical about what convicted felons tell him. But even today can you find a complete True Believer of this old kind in my native Southland.

I wish Oliver Hardy had lived to enjoy today's Southern liberals. They are so perfect they really ought to be in some kind of exhibit.

The new rich in every Southern city are desperate to prove they are not Provincial and Predictable.

As a result, Southerners who think they are Sophisticated and Original are the world's most provincial and predictable people.

Every statement a Southerner makes to show he is Unprovincial and Unpredictable comes through the same pipeline:

1) The New York Times said it two weeks ago;

2) The Atlanta Journal said it last week;

3) The local newspaper, which is part of a national chain, said it this morning, and

4) It is the Southern Sophisticate's Independent Thought for today.

Those who reside outside the South are going to think I am exaggerating. I admit that Southern liberals are people you have to see to believe. They make a snake handlers tent revival sound like a scholarly discussion.

The reason the Southern nouveau-riche are such throwbacks goes right back to Hardy's Law.

There was always hope that the little Laurel character in Laurel and Hardy would learn something, because he knew he wasn't bright. To be hopelessly stupid you have to be like Hardy and think you are a genius.

It is the Religious Inquisitor, who genuinely believes that he stands between the Heretic and Hellfire, who can be completely without the slightest trace of mercy. It is the professor, who honestly believes he represents The Only True Education, who will destroy any hint of independent thought on campus. It is the "professional reporter," who thinks only he knows what True Hard Reality is, who builds those monumental palaces in Fantasyland.

Professors, the media, all the groups the Southern New Rich worship, are agreed that only one minority is truly despicable, the Southern white man.
Many liberals have mentioned this, but the fact that
they have noticed this prejudice certainly has not
stamped it out.

The Southern liberal is a walking, talking comedy precisely because he thinks he is the Only True
Sophisticate in his region. His professors told him
so. The media told him so.

Anybody can be a hick. But the Southern "sophisticate" is a Hopeless Hick.

It Is Time For Laughter, It Is Time For Fury

Joe Sobran said in the Foreword that this book is an odd combination of white hot outrage and uproarious laughter. I began the book by pointing out what happened when I first heard the Preamble to the Soviet Constitution:

"The Union of Soviet Socialist Republics is a nation of workers, soldiers, farmers, and intellectuals."

In other words, the soldiers would die, workers would work, peasants would toil in the mud to grow food, and the intellectuals would sit on their rumps and order everybody else around. I thought it was hilarious that people would fall for that!

So I laughed.

Around me, all was silence. I suddenly got that feeling one often gets when he accidentally makes a joke to a stupid humorless person. You've been there. You make a joke, and the person stares at you with that cowlike, uncomprehending look. You get the impression that in a few seconds he is actually going to grow horns and go "Moo!"

There was nothing funny about what the "intellectuals" who brought the Soviet Union into existence actually did. Lenin and Trotsky and Mao and the rest caused at least a hundred million PEACE-TIME deaths, and even more suffering. But that still does not detract from the sheer hilariousness of the crap they sold the world.

I would do anything I could to have been able to stop those animals for the sake of humanity. But I also need to laugh at them to save my own sanity.

Saint Thomas More pointed out how effective laughter is at exposing and punishing pure evil:

"The Devil, proud spirit, cannot bear to be mocked."

At the end of "The Emperor's New Clothes," when a little child says what everybody sees, that the Emperor is marching proudly along buck naked, the crowd laughs.

But who were they laughing at?   They paid for the Emperor's nonexistent suit of clothes. They stood there admiring those nonexistent beautiful clothes until the child spoke up.

If the makers of The Emperor's New Clothes got caught after His Majesty's nakedness was exposed, I doubt that what happened to them was funny.

All the horror of Communism happened because no one saw how silly it was. All through the Cold War, I lived in a world of cows. In that classroom, nobody saw the joke.   Liberals fell for the idea that intellectuals would sit on their asses and give orders. Conservatives argued with Marxists as if they were saying something serious. The idea that an economy owned and run by bureaucrats will be efficient is insane.

You don't argue with insanity. If an insane person is harmless, you see the humor in it. If he gets like Lenin, you lock him up. But no sane person argues with a laughable nutcase.

The Catholic Church is, to say the least, a highly competent organization. Any bishop in America who did not know that little boys were being molested on a vast scale in the 1970s would have to be deaf and a moron.

So the bishops say, 1) We didn't know anything about it, and 2) The reason we did nothing about it is because the social scientists back then said we should just reform the molesters.

That is like the defense lawyer who says, 1) My client didn't do it and 2) My client was insane when he performed the act.

So the bishops are both funny and criminal.

Social scientists who push one horribly disastrous policy after another should have been objects of laughter long since. They said criminals were really sweeties who had been mistreated. They said an economy owned and run by bureaucrats would be wildly efficient. I heard them say that. I heard them teach that. I heard their students say those things. And I saw people die and lives ruined.

To say that lifetime criminals are really sweeties who should be out on the streets should be laughed at. It wasn't. The judge who put a hundred criminals out on the streets was far more criminal than any of them. The bishop who foisted twenty child-molesting priests on one community after another is more guilty than any of the child molesters.

I think that enough little boys have had their lives ruined by those pervert priests the bishops thought were basically good guys. I think enough innocent people have been murdered and raped and crippled by repeat offenders put back on the streets by people who said they were basically sweet kids.

For God's sake, it is time we learned the two lessons of The Emperor's New Clothes:

Lesson One:

We look at how stupid we have been and laugh at everybody who fell for that crap.

Lesson II:

We catch those bastards and do something to them that is very, very unfunny indeed.